11|3

CW01640538

Andy and Me:
A Life for My Disabled Son

By

Barbara O'Donnell

ISBN: 978-1-8380464-2-2

Published By: -

i2i PUBLISHING

i2i Publishing. Manchester.

www.i2ipublishing.co.uk

I'd like to dedicate this book to my children and all the staff that have supported Andy over the last twenty-two years.

Acknowledgements

I'd like to thank Dr Peter Fox (now retired) and Dinah Robinson, the then Community Support Nurse, as the only health professionals that believed in me and the company.

Without that support, I would not have been able to carry on and this book wouldn't have been written.

Contents

6

Prologue

An Underrated Job

Being a mother is an underrated job by most agencies. If your child is not perfect in health or physicality, it is still almost regarded as a shame. I bring to mind my dog being petted by some people with learning disabilities with their carers the other day. As they went to leave, the carers said 'Thank-you', as if it was a rare thing to be treated as another passing member of society.

I understood though, as I've worked in care for over thirty years. There is still the 'Does he take sugar?' attitude towards the person with disabilities, with the attention given to their carers, rather than to the person themselves.

As a parent of a child and young adult with learning and physical disabilities, you become over-protective at first, ready to see a slight or a snigger in other peoples' attitudes. Then, over time, you learn that this is the norm and to get on with it. Most member of the public have been great, but some have not.

The idea for the book was with me for quite a few years. The helpful health professionals that are mentioned in the book (Dr Peter Fox and Dinah Robinson) had often said to me that I should do something like this, as it would perhaps get information out to other parents in similar situations. We were all aware that there were many other parents out there not being taken seriously, being thought of as being too emotionally involved to make a rational decision about their offspring or being thought to be thick because they are mum.

Therefore, I hope that the book may help those parents who feel intimidated by healthcare staff or doctors and feel powerless to question their decisions, which they may not agree with.

I had not written a book before, so just started writing things down as a record of our experiences with Andy. No one helped me; I just wrote what I thought was relevant to tell the story.

As time passed, there were more and more sections written down and the real possibility that these could be combined into a book, became a reality.

Now that it has been published, my hopes for the book itself are really to be a guide to encourage other parents with a child (or an adult) who has disabilities. I think it's important for parents to remember not to listen too much to what the professional says (unless it is about a physical condition). It is the parents who know their own child. They are the experts on how their child behaves as they have lived with him or her for years on a twenty-four-hour basis - and not the swiftly trained pen-pusher.

The book is also for the siblings of disabled individuals It's not just the parent and disabled person who are affected by the situation. It is difficult for the siblings of the disabled child or adult are involved and have their lives affected by what is going on. Sadly, they too will get bullied and mocked. This happened to mine, who, I'm glad to say, have always stuck up for themselves – and Andy. They are my greatest achievement.

Chapter 1

The Wrong Diagnosis

12

Medical Negligence

Andy was born on the thirtieth of October 1979 and was a perfect baby boy. He became a jolly, well-fed, healthy, intelligent baby until he was fifteen months old, when he contracted meningitis. My doctor had told me it was influenza – there was a local epidemic at the time in the Medway Towns, so I believed him. As a family, we thought we had been lucky to get on Dr Khan's NHS list, as every doctor in the area was over-subscribed because of the influx of Londoners - we'd moved from Clapham - who were wanting cheaper and better accommodation, better schools and less violence (these were the days of moral panic about street muggings).

We didn't know it at the time, but Dr Khan was also over-subscribed. Andy had no rash classically symptomatic of meningitis, but he seemed to shiver all the time which I took to be part of his fever. I had been told, wrongly, to keep him warm by Dr Khan. Reversely, I should have been keeping him as *cool* as possible: this 'keeping him warm' accelerated Andy's condition.

In fact, his 'shivering' was constant fitting (epilepsy) because of his high temperature: I had no previous knowledge of fits and would only have recognised classic, as-seen-on-film flailing limbs or violent twitching. But I did know that high temperatures were dangerous. I was worried enough to call out a locum during the night of the first day of his illness. Apparently, the locum prescribed the entirely wrong medication; it again accelerated Andy's condition, instead of containing it. On the second day, I telephoned Dr Khan who asked me to bring him to the surgery. It was the fifteenth of January 1981 and snowing heavily. I asked him if he would do a home visit instead, and he reluctantly agreed. He literally 'popped' in, glanced at Andy and said that as a young mum, I was being over-protective and too emotional, probably because my hormones were running amok (I was pregnant with my third child). He said Andy was fine and would soon get better. He did not examine him. I took the doctor at his word.

It was the next day at home when Andy's breathing became shallow and his eyes rolled backwards into his head. I informed Dr Khan who said I should call an ambulance. He met me at the hospital, and in front of the two ambulance men who escorted me into the hospital (no doubt seeing them as potential witnesses, as he knew he'd fucked-up royally) said, "Mrs O'Donnell, why did you leave it so long?" I was too shocked to speak as the enormity of the situation was beginning to dawn upon me. Andy was whipped away for a lumbar puncture and later, we found that he had contracted bacterial meningitis. We didn't know it at the time, but he would be permanently, profoundly brain-damaged, physically disabled with hemiplegia to the whole right side of his body, and as a side-effect of the brain damage, would have acute epilepsy and would go on to have extreme challenging behaviour.

Andy spent three days at All Saints Hospital, Chatham, where he almost died twice and 'fitted' constantly. Because of this fitting, and its association with the high temperatures which Andy was running, all the windows were kept open to cool him down. This was the middle of January. As a result of his exposure to the cold air, Andy developed pneumonia. He was referred to Great Ormond Street Children's Hospital, as Chatham could no longer offer Andy any medical aid. There, he received the brain scan which confirmed the amount of damage the meningitis had done.

I had to wait outside the theatre (I couldn't risk any radiation damage to the unborn baby I was carrying) whilst he went in with the medical staff. When they eventually came out, I didn't have to ask for their professional opinion. The medical practitioner; floppy-haired, upper-crust, pinstripe-suited, bow-tied and intimidating, who *possibly* did not realise I was Andy's mum, (who else would I have been?) but announced loudly and plummily anyway that, "This one will be lucky if he does anything, practically a vegetable!...about three-quarters gone." His meaning was clear: three quarters of Andy's brain had effectively been destroyed by meningitis. Comments like this, however unwitting, either bring you to your knees whilst eating Valium, or make you tough and aggressive. I was going to have to go the tough route for the sake of Andy and my other children.

Harsh Reality

At Great Ormond Street Hospital, their policy is to cater for all denominations for the comfort of the patient and their family. It was increasingly obvious that Andy would never be the same again, so I did not welcome the attentions of the priest – probably attracted by my Irish surname – who asked if I would like to pray with him. This may be of great comfort to committed Christians. However, on this occasion, I told him no - not unless he could turn the clock back or perform miracles. I queried what sort of God destroyed the lives of innocent babies, obviously not the 'God of Love' I had been led to believe he was and asked the priest in no uncertain terms to leave the room.

My behaviour was not very kind, I realise, but the priest was probably the last person who could have comforted me. As far as I was concerned, he had very little experience of a mother's relationship with her child. For me, at that time, it just brought the futility of my situation home and made me angry with what seemed to be the false hope of organised religion.

From that time on, I was determined that I was going to treat Andy as 'normally' as possible. I had no previous experience of disability, there was none in the family that I could remember, but I was well aware of its social stigma: of its association with deviance, and the pity and charitable feelings that a disabled baby or child brought out in others and conversely, the repulsion that was universally felt for a disabled adult. There was the strange shame that it seemed to bring upon a family and, naturally, the general exclusion from ordinary society as a result of disability. I determined that this was never going to be the case for me.

For a fleeting moment, I remembered the coachloads of young adults with downs syndrome living in care that holidayed in Blackpool, where I grew up, who were all dressed the same - in old man's belted mackintoshes and flat-caps regardless of age; all the same but very different from us. As a child, I had been intrigued by them but had been told to keep away from the 'Mongols' because they were well-known for being highly sexed. It was a shame, they couldn't help it, but stay away all the same.

Andy was not going to be different. He would be fully included in every aspect of family life and treated exactly like the other children. He would be loved and cared for and I was going to show all the doubters who thought that it would be too much for me just how wrong they were. There would be no allowances for his condition, whatever that might be; of course, I was young, hopeful and could not envisage the future.

Andy was discovered to have meningitis on the sixteenth of January 1981. I was five months pregnant with what would be my third child, Bobby. My eldest child was

Caroline at four years old and two years later, I would give birth to Tommy. I had absolutely no idea of the prejudice, sheer hard-work, violence and heartbreak that was to come. If I had known, I would probably have unplugged Andy's life support machine at All Saints Hospital when I first got the diagnosis for the sake of my other children, (and me) because of how it would affect our lives. But as a young mother, with no experience of profound disability, giving up on my child was not an option. Andy was well-loved – the cliché, 'Where there's life, there's hope' was perfectly true.

Going Home

Great Ormond Street Hospital sent Andy back home. There was nothing they could do for him. I had asked the doctor for an honest diagnosis, and not to 'kid-glove' me because I was pregnant. I was not going to break down - I just wanted to know what I was in for. He said that the best recovery after brain damage through meningitis would be in the first six months, then a slower progress over the next two years, and after that period of time any progress would be a bonus. I thanked him for his honesty; if I didn't know the truth or the prognosis, how on earth could I try to help my son?

When I carried Andy through the door at home on that first day back, he did the strangest thing. His favourite nursery rhyme had been 'Hot Cross Buns' and he used to sing the first three notes with me - 'duh duh der'. That first day, he sang 'duh duh der' constantly, repetitively about five times in a row; then never again for years. Encouraged by this recognition, I pointed to the electric light at the top of the stairs, which he had tried to name as a fifteen-month old. In his mouth it had sounded like 'la'- and he actually said 'la', just once this time, and then, nothing. No more speech until he was just over three years old.

My dad came to stay for a few weeks on Andy's release from hospital. My mum had been here for Caroline whilst I spent my days, and my husband Steve spent the nights, by Andy's bedside, so they were going to change about. I realised, because I had been told, that the after-service from the hospital would start as soon as Andy was released home. Previous to the meningitis, I had never received any visits from the local health visitor. I'd always had to make the trip to the clinic. Andy had only been home one day when I answered the door to not one, but three, health visitors, all curious to see Andy. I was furious. I calmly said, "Come to see the crippled idiot, have you? Why don't you all fuck off?"

My dad, ex-Durham miner as a boy, ex-navy in World War Two, and retired fireman (and no stranger to swearing), was horrified. I was speaking to professional people with no respect. Worse, I sounded 'common', something that he had tried to escape from since leaving home at eighteen to join up. I know that he felt ashamed of me. I also knew though, that this behaviour and hardening of my feelings would only increase as I fought my son's corner.

After two weeks had passed, I asked dad if he would go back home to Blackpool (no offence meant and hopefully, none taken) – I needed to be able to get on with this situation by myself, and not rely on others. I didn't want to become dependent on others to help me to cope on a day-to-day basis. He only went when I promised I would ask for help if I needed it. I agreed. I wouldn't ask for help, though: I needed to be able to cope alone as my husband worked in London in the music business. We had only moved to Kent fourteen months earlier, when Andy was five weeks old, because property was affordable, the schools were better than in Clapham and the children would have more freedom to roam.

My husband, a talented musician, songwriter and record producer, had a very social job, based in London. Meetings would take place in pubs, clubs and restaurants, and alcohol was a big part of the culture (as were recreational drugs).To mask the hurt, and possibly the shame, of having seen his first, perfect son transformed into a disabled child, his alcohol capacity was stepped up to a level that would best be described as dipsomania. He would go for benders lasting up to three days then be health conscious, anti-alcohol and play squash for the next week. This behaviour got progressively worse.

Chapter 2

The New Andy

Repetitive Routine

I needed to be able to manage alone. As time passed, I devised a routine that was almost compulsive in its repetition. I had to. I had my eldest child at play school three mornings a week, (Monday, Wednesday and Friday) Andy at the 'special' play school at Parkwood twice a week (Tuesday and Thursday), where the special bus came to pick him up at the designated time, and a new baby to look after (born five months after Andy's meningitis). I had deliberately arranged the days like this so that Caroline and Bobby could have time without Andy.

I also had to cope with other people's ignorance of the consequences of meningitis itself, or sometimes just plain ignorance. "Oh, he's a big strong boy, he'll soon get better," was a favourite – proving that when people ask how you (or in this case Andy) are, they are not listening to the answer because they're really not interested. A classic gaff was when asked why Andy had been in hospital - and been told he'd had meningitis, the reply was, 'I had laryngitis recently, it was nasty, but he'll be fine in time.'(Christ!)

I wondered how they could fail to notice the stroke-like paralysis of his face, his slowly atrophying right arm, his fist of a right hand and the way he was in a pram all the time slumped forward or to one side, as he could no longer sit-up for himself. Did they not see the pink, padded helmet he was forced to wear because of the frequency and severity of his epileptic fits, or even the fits themselves (the noise Andy made on the onset of a fit was like an animal in pain, a low growling noise which swelled into a full-blown howl), or indeed, the fits themselves, where the right arm and leg swung across his body and violently twitched and his face contorted as if it was being pulled downwards by an invisible hand? These symptoms were never commented on, except by true friends. The embarrassment of disability was so real, you could almost feel it in solid form.

This is not to say that all our neighbours were ignorant or unhelpful. Most were really helpful, did listen and empathised without making me, Steve, Caroline or Andy (Bobby was too young to have an opinion) feel like objects of pity. Our neighbours were like those described by people who had lived through World War Two. Before my mum and dad came to help out, neighbours were picking Steve up at 5.30a.m. from All Saints Hospital, Chatham, bringing him home from the hospital where he'd been all night. I was waiting, ready to go, at home. He'd come home to be with Caroline, and I'd go back to the hospital to be with Andy, ferried by a neighbour. Caroline was looked after by neighbours, and played and had tea with their children – they were fantastic.

Early Progress

Andy was visited by a physiotherapist once a week who showed me how to manipulate his limbs so that they would remain supple and she suggested I put some noise device onto his right wrist, as Andy's brain at present did not recognise his right side, but with constant reminders, it just might. I tied a small bell with a bright blue ribbon onto his right wrist and tried to make him notice his right side. For example, I'd sit on his right side all the time so that he would have to turn to notice where mum's voice was coming from. I always held onto his right hand, not his left. I would set the table as if he had two working hands, with a spoon and fork, and would balance the fork in his right hand. I would try to emphasise his right side and manipulated it constantly because it was already showing signs of curvature and muscle wastage.

At this time, Andy couldn't walk; in fact, the doctors had indicated that if he did walk, it would be by means of sticks or a frame. I used to have a futon - low to the ground, with a wooden frame - where I would balance Andy standing (or slumped) over the couch with his arms both hooked over the arm of the futon and bribe him with all sorts of goodies to stay standing. He would fall after a few minutes and cry, so after lots of praise and treats we'd start again. I often had to go to the kitchen, where I could see him, but he couldn't see me and cry at his bravery. I didn't even know if I was being cruel, I just wanted him to reach his full potential. The doctor's prophetic words haunted me - "the best progress will be in the first six months, then there will be slower progress over the next two years, then anything after that will be a bonus" - I didn't feel I could afford to waste a moment of the next precious two and a half years, so I didn't.

What was noticeable at this time was the alarming change in his behaviour. Before meningitis, Andy had been very jolly, with a really infectious or as others had noted, a 'dirty' laugh, but loud noises like the hoover, or a sudden ambulance siren would scare him to tears. He was a good sleeper with a sweet nature. After some recovery, about five or six months after his illness (when Bobby was a new baby), his behaviour was almost the complete opposite of his old self. Even though he could only shuffle across the floor on his bottom, pulling himself along with his left hand, he was usually going towards an object he could break, and at an unbelievable speed considering his disabilities. He broke three 'unbreakable' Fisher Price Jack-in-a-box's (noisy by themselves) within two months by beating them relentlessly with a squeaky hammer. The noise, coupled with his laughing at the destruction and the other children trying to compete over the noise, was LOUD.

This floor progression was not limited to toys as the object of his attention. People: babies, adults, old people, teenagers or any living creature: dogs, cats, other family pets, flies, wasps, bees, frogs - the list goes on – were all targeted to be attacked and hurt. We were beginning to realise that this was not the gentle, cuddly Andy of old. If we had been a family living a few hundred years before, we would have believed our son's soul had been possessed by the Devil and would have had him exorcised by a priest. However, knowing what we did, we realised the old Andy was, in some ways, dead. This new Andy just looked like him but had nothing in common with the baby we had loved. This was a bereavement – which I had no time to indulge myself in - and a getting-to-know-again process.

Dad's Health

It was around this time that my father suddenly became poorly. The previous May (1982), he'd had a strange period of breathlessness. He'd felt physically weak, he couldn't get up without real effort and seemed to be gasping for breath. This passed, and he was soon back to normal – or so I thought; it's hard to gauge what's actually happening over the phone, especially when people "don't want to worry you" because "you've got enough on."

I decided to pay a visit. Caroline, Andy, Bobby and I went to Blackpool for a few days: we were hardly ever accompanied by Steve. When I saw dad, I noticed how parchment-like his usually dark skin was and how yellow the whites of his eyes were, even more so than normal.(Dad had been posted to Singapore during World War Two and had contracted jaundice out there, which left the whites of his eyes discoloured anyway). When he accompanied me with the children on days out, he was really breathless, but I put this down to the aftermath of his mystery illness. I returned to Kent with my mind at rest about dad.

Five months later, on Friday the eighth of October 1982, my sister Joan phoned at teatime, telling me that dad been admitted to hospital. Again, he was gasping for breath. Only days before, he had driven her boys to school, so we both didn't realise the seriousness of his condition. Joan asked me what I thought she should take him, by way of distraction, at visiting time. I said, "The latest Jackie Collins book and chocolate," which she agreed with. He liked the racy-ness of Jackie Collins and loved chocolate: it wouldn't have occurred to him that it might have looked a bit 'soft' reading what would be perceived as a woman's book whilst eating chocolate! He didn't care - he was too macho for that. At seven-thirty the same evening, I received another phone call, again from Joan. As she'd arrived at the ward, clutching the Jackie Collins' book and chocolate, she'd walked right into the scenario of my dad being given a heart resuscitation, which failed shortly after, with mum sitting in an ante-ward in shock.

Dad was dead. He was only sixty-four and had been a brilliant dad and devoted granddad. He'd been so worried about Andy's future, and the fact that I was pregnant yet again. From a family of nine children himself (it would have been eleven but two died as babies) he saw large families as a poverty trap which he'd escaped from. Both he and mum (one of five kids) thought that having more than two children as pretty stupid. I was five months pregnant with Tommy, number four, when he died.

Chapter 3

Fits and Shouts

First Words

I was lucky enough to have a good consultant at All Saints Hospital, where Andy was an out-patient for the next three years. He clearly explained all the changes that had happened to Andy as a consequence of his damaged brain in terms that I could understand and try to address. A year had passed, when Andy began to make strange guttural noises to try to communicate in words, which was wonderful. None of these sounds resembled any of the words that I constantly repeated to him. It was at this stage that Bobby, aged one, regarding Andy as his older, wiser brother, would copy his speech. This was very frustrating. They could communicate between themselves, but everyone else perceived their communication as gobbledegook.

I wanted Andy to be able to speak his name ('O'Donnell' eventually came out quite aggressively as 'Adowa'), followed by his address - it was always a possibility that he could get lost, or be snatched by a stranger - all sorts of unthinkable notions would go through my mind because of his vulnerability.

By the time Andy was three, he was able to make himself understood and spoke the odd word clearly. He still had his own versions of words, though. On a family break to Blackpool, Andy's cousins Paul, Danny and Jamie came around to Grandma's house to see us all. They had brought a friend called Trevor with them and whilst all the kids were playing in Grandma's garden, Andy, at the same time as charging around the garden at an angle, was trying to say Trevor's name, as it was a name he wasn't familiar with. He thought that he's got it - but it came out sounding like Chobabeebee - much to the hysteria of the other kids (the name apparently stuck with poor Trevor for a while).

Andy still wore his bell on his right arm because his 'centre' was still between his left ear and the left side of his nose. He still had to be constantly reminded of his right-side. He was also walking with the aid of a specially-made-for-him calliper which was Velcro-ed to his right leg. Although he was now walking, he tired easily, so I used a double buggy for him and Bobby, which collectively, weighed a ton. Caroline would hold onto the pram and Billy the dog would have his lead slipped on to the other pram handle with the shopping. I was now six months pregnant with Tommy.

This speaking started, almost properly, on a late November afternoon in 1982, one month after my dad had died. It was a memorable evening in two ways. I had taken the children to the park, Bobby, a baby of seventeen months and Caroline (who had just had her birthday) was six. A little boy of about seven was also on the park - alone - and it was just becoming twilight, so I felt concerned for him. I was helping Bobby and Andy on the see-saw. I had to split my time between them because Andy weighed far more than Bob, so I had to stop Bobby flying off and Andy couldn't hold on properly, so I had to hold him on. Caroline was on the swings and Billy, the dog, was sniffing around the park. Whilst I was holding on to Bobby, Andy started to have a grand mal fit and fell off the see-saw to the ground.

Before I could get Bob off the see-saw and see to Andy, the little boy on the park ran towards Andy and started to quite viciously kick him, all the while shouting that he was a "fuckin' freak" and laughing at him. I was totally shocked for a few seconds, and then I quite literally saw red. I lumbered pregnant across to him and cracked him across the shoulders to get him off my son. He screamed, "I'm goin' get my mum to fuckin' hit you back!" I was so angry, that I didn't stop to think of the wrongness of what I'd done. I said "Go on then, you little shit – I'd like to see what kind of bitch brought you up. I'll wait here – go on…get her!"

Andy's fit was slowly subsiding, they lasted about two to three minutes then, and eventually he seemed alright, if a little tired, which is how they left him. (I found out later at bath time that this time he was also bruised to the body). Sometimes, he'd wet or mess himself, or be physically sick but fortunately, not this time, so I waited. It got darker, and colder, but I still waited. When it was obvious that nobody was coming, I went home, slightly disappointed and very upset. Even though I was pregnant, I wanted to kill the mother or father that had brought up a little person to think like this. I felt no shred of shame for hitting the child – he had hit and kicked my disabled son in the midst of an epileptic seizure – as far as I was concerned at the time, rightly or wrongly, the child deserved it.

As I was rounding all the children up to go home, I held Andy and pointed at the moon. As I always did, I said "moon" and to my joy he said "moon" back – not perfectly clearly, but identifiably, definitely, "moon". It was Andy's first proper word.

Even Louder Speech

This, in some ways, became a double-edged sword because, once Andy found that he had a voice, he used it from the moment he woke up (in the early hours) until he went to bed at 7.30p.m. He started as he meant to go on all day, that is, by shouting at the top of his voice. This started at 3.30a.m. with him bawling, "MUM!... MUMMY!" at the top of his voice, which made sure that I got up with him, and of course I did. I didn't want the other children to wake up too. Andy's normal speaking voice was, by most people's standards a loud shout.

As time passed, the consultant thought that his ears may have been affected by meningitis, so he went through all the tests for finding whether there was a hearing impairment. They all proved negative, so there was nothing wrong with his ears, which was good, giving me one less thing to worry about. His eyesight was fine, too. That had been established by extensive tests – also good news. He hardly ever caught a cold either (only major illnesses were good enough for Andy). I got really sick of people telling me that he would be fine in time because he was a big, strong boy! What on earth has physical strength got to do with brain damage?

By the summer, Andy was walking with a pronounced limp, but he was walking unaided which was wonderful. He tired easily so I still had to have the double buggy with me, which wasn't a problem as I had to have it with me anyway – Tommy wasn't even one year old yet. When I went out shopping with the kids I had Bobby and Andy in the double buggy, Caroline holding the pram on one side, Billy, the dog, on the other side of the pram, shopping bags on the pram handles and Tommy strapped in a baby-sling on the front of my body! I used to get disapproving *"tut-tuts"* from elderly women and comments from men like *"No tele in your house, then?"* Great.

Although Andy's right leg had made some progress, his right foot turned inwards, and he walked on the inside of his foot. Similarly, his right arm had progressed – his right elbow was a lethal weapon, but his right hand had to be manipulated constantly and was permanently clenched. His fingers had no use: basically, his brain was telling him he had no right hand or working fingers, so that was that for his hand, although I carried on trying to make it work. Andy would hold his useless right hand with his left hand when he was standing still and with his dark good looks, he attracted lots of attention, not all of it positive.

It was at this time that it was impossible to ignore other people's reaction to his shouting, his blue ribbon with the bell attached, and his calliper. Some people either ignored him even if he was trying to communicate with them or openly gawped at him, especially when he was having one of his vocal epileptic fits in public.

On one occasion, Andy, Bobby, Tommy and I were waiting for Caroline in the school playground. What had happened to Andy was common knowledge in the school playground and most people made a real fuss of him. He would run around the playground at a crazy angle and try to speak to people. This particular time, Andy limped up to a little girl about his own age. Her mother grabbed her and pushed the little girl behind her, in effect hiding her.

Andy was just being friendly – at this time, I could tell if he was going to launch himself at someone – so her behaviour was hurtful: but given his increasingly violent behaviour, I suppose, was totally understandable. I led him away from the woman, saying fairly loudly, "Don't worry, it's not catching." I felt, as most parents of children with disabilities do, that I had to fight that bit extra on behalf of Andy - and as a result, my feelings were raw and hardened against what I perceived to be negative criticism.

Extreme Fits

There have been many, many times when people have just openly stopped and stared when Andy had a fit in a public space and only a small minority have asked if I needed some help. The rest seemed to think that it didn't matter if they stared, that for some reason known only to them that this difference in behaviour justified their attention, like a freak show put on for their benefit. Again, in retrospect, they were probably shocked into standing and staring by the spectacle of Andy twitching violently whilst making his bull-elephant noise. Whatever their reasons for gazing, they did not go down well with me. If people continued to stare, I'd ask them to fuck-off, unless they thought they could help.

Andy's fits were a major cause for concern. He was having seven or more grand mal fits a day, which was not good for the state of his brain, his physical health or his personality – the old-fashioned belief of 'epileptic rage' was recognisable in his escalating violence. Medication after medication was tried out on him but they did nothing to lessen the fits. What they did do was make him dozy in the daytime and awake all night – a complete nightmare for all of us. A specialist diet from Great Ormond Street Hospital was even tried, where our concerned consultant at All Saints Hospital had referred us back to. The special diet consisted of lamb, potatoes prepared in any way, rice cakes, oil but no saturated fats or dairy produce and some green vegetables. Andy was the envy of the other kids because he could have unlimited chips if he didn't want any of the other limited, fairly boring foods on the diet – the only time I'd allowed him special treatment. At this stage, it was anything to reduce the fits, as they were becoming life-threatening.

It wasn't just the amount of time that Andy was unconscious that made the fits life-threatening. It was how suddenly, where and how he fell when he had a 'drop' fit. There were many, many occasions where he hurt himself badly but two memorably really bad incidents. One was whilst Andy was asleep. At about 12.30a.m., we woke to hear Andy's distinctive fitting noise and found that he had got stuck between the bed and the radiator (which was turned up fairly high to keep his right side warm).The skin of his right ear was stuck to the radiator and the whole shell of the ear was burnt by the time we'd safely freed him. When it healed, the ear was permanently misshapen.

The other time happened outside my front door where I was unloading some shopping from the pram. Bobby and Andy were play fighting - pushing and shoving each other - when Andy went into a grand mal fit and landed the back of his head on the corner of the wall with a crack; splitting it open. I had not put on his distinctive, pink padded helmet on that day because he had been mostly sat in the pram, so I felt entirely responsible. He had to have twelve stitches to the back of his head later that day.

Shortly after this time (March 1984), we moved to Gillingham to a larger house, a total necessity. Caroline was seven, Andy was four, Bobby was a few months off three and Tommy was one. Our first house in Kent had been a two bedroomed cottage in Rainham: not good when you have two adults, four children, one intent on killing everything in his wake, and a dog. It was in Gillingham that I realised that it was make-or-break-time for my marriage. Steve could no longer stand the noise, the worry about Andy's future, the responsibilities of being a father and the very early mornings - it also clashed with his drinking and socialising timetable. He began drinking more, coming home less, and staying in London even more. This was of no help to Andy or the other children, or me. He obviously was not happy, and I certainly wasn't.

Holiday Getaway

Things were getting worse at home so I decided to go to my mum's in Blackpool every chance I could to get away from the unpredictability and uncertainty of the situation. (Steve only came home three or four times a week and was always drunk when he did turn up). I began to go 'on holiday' more and more - at Christmas, Easter and Summer school holidays - always taking the dog with me because I had no money for kennels and Steve refused to look after him. I'd had enough of the home situation, Caroline loved to play with her cousins, the boys loved the beach and mum was lonely, so it was ideal.

It was the summer of 1985. I decided that I'd take Andy and Tommy as a two-year old to see Disney's Pinocchio, because it was doing the rounds in cinemas again. I'd already seen the film as a child, but I thought that Andy (who loved music) and Tommy might enjoy it. Joan had agreed to have Caroline and Bobby for the afternoon. I had no car, so I had to bus to Joan's first, then bus into town to the Odeon Cinema (now Funny Girls) where Pinocchio was showing. So far, so good! Everything went really well - Tommy was sat on my knee and Andy was really liking the colours and songs - until I heard the familiar sound of the beginning of an onset grand mal seizure.

Andy was making the animal noise that heralded a seizure. It was loud and people were turning in their seats to see what was going on. I had to stop him from falling off the cinema seat which, being a flip-up seat, was unstable anyway. I tried to put his head into my chest so that the noise would be less. I was also holding onto Tommy who was getting agitated too. People were shushing me and Jiminy Cricket was singing *When you wish upon a star*. It occurred to me in that moment that the last time I'd seen the film was with my dad and Joan at the same cinema when I was about five-years old. Fortunately, Andy's fit eventually abated, I apologised to all the people I'd disturbed - and it was dark so no one could see me crying. I still can't hear that song without tears.

Chapter 4

Blackpool Beckons

Planned Escape

I began to realise that my marriage was over. I knew that the children would have a better life if we lived in Blackpool. The schools were better, they had all the beach to play on, their Grandma (my mum; she thought that 'Nana' sounded like the hired help), Nana (Steve's mum), Auntie Joan and cousins were there – it seemed to make sense that if I was going to get a divorce, then Blackpool was the place to be for family support. I would have a willing baby-sitter in my mum, who was at a bit of a loose-end since the death of my dad, and I could work at night time for the extra money, which I was going to need.

It took me until the twenty-third of May 1986 to finally get to Blackpool. I had found a house near schools, a Sainsbury's, a park, a school and the beach – ideal! – and, on one of my 'holidays', after an unbelievable struggle, I actually did it. That entailed: lots of deception, lies, travelling on a coach with all the children and the dog from Gillingham, having to change at Victoria Coach Station for the coach to Blackpool, then get to my mother's house in Norbreck to deposit the children, then going to the estate agent for the key and getting to the new address before the removal men arrived, unpack and move in then make something to eat for the kids for when the grandmas brought them back.

I wanted everything to be normal for them: I wanted all their belongings to be unpacked and in their rooms for when they arrived – and it was, and I did it. Fortunately, my sister had helped me; she'd had until three o'clock, then she had to go because her kids were coming back from school. I even assembled bunk beds. It's amazing what you can do when you really have to. No stress then! Our new house, Red Bank Road in Bispham, was smaller than the old house in Gillingham, but

I loved it because I was now independent, and I felt it was all mine.

A drunken husband, when you've got four children, and especially when one of them is as difficult to manage as Andy was, is no husband at all.

New Schools

My sister had helped me to enrol the kids into the local schools and had even gone to a tribunal on my behalf to get one of them into an oversubscribed school which was just around the corner. I had no car at this stage, I couldn't even drive. Fortunately, the schools were all walking distance except Andy's - but he of course had the special bus which came at 8.20a.m. Perfect for me, as I had lots of time to make sure the other children got to school on time.

The only special school in the area was Highfurlong School and the intake was a real mix of children and young people with varying disabilities. As Andy was only nearly seven years old (this was May and his birthday was October) he was still an infant in school terms. The infant campus was in Singleton Hall, a beautiful old manor house in extensive grounds. On parents' days, you could hear the pheasants calling outside - idyllic. It could also be said that it was far away from mainstream school and completely exclusive from normal society, hidden where it was at Singleton. However, it was a really good school, with a lovely headmaster, Mr Roberts, who knew all the children's names, and all about them.

None of the other children were like Andy. He had to have a 1:1 member of staff with him at all times for the safety of the other children. He was growing quite tall and was big for his age. His fits were still as bad as ever. Considering the amount of brain damage incurred with the meningitis, he did very well at school. His concentration skills were impaired, he was easily distracted, his motor skills were greatly damaged because of his hemiplegia and if Andy couldn't be bothered to do something, or someone tried to make him participate, they would suffer through his violent outbursts.

At this stage, Andy would do more for me than he would for his teachers, so I decided to help out once a week at Highfurlong with reading practice. He had learned his colours, his alphabet and his numbers up to twenty at home before he went to school, as had my other children. They could all read and write before they went to school, and fortunately they all did well at school, another thing not to worry about.

Mr. Men and Lego

Andy had displayed obsessional behaviour for some time. I was not particularly concerned because at least he was showing an interest in certain things: Mr. Men books, Ladybird books, notably Nursery Rhymes (he loved music and would do a lop-sided dance when he heard something he liked then) 'Duplo' (big) Lego, wooden coloured bricks (a.k.a. lethal weapons) and the odd cuddly toy. If Andy had been born with the disabilities that he had, he would have been pigeon-holed as classically autistic.

For example, he could look at his Lego spread out on the floor and in a glance tell you how many pieces were there, and which colours they were - and he was always right. If you asked him what number his Mr Greedy book was (all the Mr Men had a different number on the spine of the book against the name of the particular Mr Man) he immediately knew the right number. But not just Mr Greedy, all forty-three of them.

He became obsessed with mail order catalogues. Well-meaning friends would save their catalogues for Andy and as he collected more, he became more and more obsessed with them, especially the Autumn/Winter catalogues because of the pictures of chocolates and toys. Department stores own Christmas catalogues were a great favourite – everything he'd ever wanted in one book! I was convinced that the bedroom floor would collapse under the weight of his hundreds of weighty tomes. All these catalogues should have made him happy, obsessed as he was, but unfortunately for him (and us) his cognitive condition limited his ability to be happy for long periods of time. He began to rip pages out of his catalogues, therefore making his collection pages and not books, and increasing the size of the 'collection'. It was at this stage that Andy began not to be able to handle the size of the collection as it was now too big for him to cope with.

He would wake-up even earlier so that he could count the pages, getting one number wrong and starting again – an exercise in complete frustration and impotence. The sheer frustration of the situation he was in the grip of would boil over into violence, aimed at me or the other kids. At this stage, Andy did not self-harm, he just took his frustration out on whoever was the nearest to him.

Although these behaviours were sheer hard work to contain, it was still possible for me to be in control of Andy. To be part of the normal outside world was getting harder and harder as he grew and grew and became more and more powerful, I had to be there at all times. Even at the age of eight, Andy was a formidable character. He shouted, he swore, (learned from his mum, rather than killing him) he certainly wasn't shy, he would attack anybody, but sometimes could be lovable, cuddly and incredibly funny. He had (and still has) a 'sick' sense of humour. If someone tripped up and better still, hurt themselves, Andy would hoot with laughter. If he went past a dog that was squatting down for a poo, he would point and laugh his distinctive 'fat-boy' laugh.

But he had a capacity in him that could not be happy for very long. In fact, he would deliberately make himself unhappy as with his 'collections'. I have always thought that this is not just the result of having obsessional behaviour, epilepsy, frustration with his hemiplegia and profound brain damage, although these are major contributions. Andy, before meningitis, was a very bright baby and an early walker (supposedly early development is a sign of intelligence) and I believe that he was then, as he is now, clearly aware of his in-capabilities and was and is still generally unhappy with his lack of 'normality'. And I've no doubt departments in colleges teaching about social inclusion, equality and the lauding of diversity throughout the curriculum will not be happy with this personal diagnosis.

Targeted Bullying

It was whilst we were at Red Bank Road that other children noticed that Andy was not like them. In the main, the friends of my children would be understanding when we tried to explain the reasons behind the way he behaved and spoke, and they accepted him for what he was - and how he behaved. This was all positive. I was determined that Andy would be treated the same as my other children and would be included as much as possible in 'normal' life.

This was not the case when we encountered strangers in the public sphere. Adults would tut and stare, children would openly laugh at either his pronounced limp or his shouty delivery. I was often told by strangers that I should make my child behave whilst waiting in a supermarket queue – to which my reply was, 'I'm sorry, but he is disabled', which I thought was very restrained. Another of my mantras! Again, this was understandable behaviour looking back at the times where disability was not particularly seen – let alone heard - and I think that society has come a long way in the last thirty or so years: just not yet far enough.

My children have all defended Andy when their friends or schoolchildren have made fun of him. Either by physical means or by insults. I have had stand-up arguments with parents of those children because of my refusal to apologise for my children's behaviour or make them apologise. I would question their parental skills instead and ask if it was normal for them to call disabled children 'spastics, window-lickers, mongs' etc. as their children had clearly got this language from somewhere (or them) – and had not been corrected if they said offensive words.

As a parent, it is the most hurtful experience to have your disabled child laughed at or looked down upon. It is bad enough when your children are able-bodied and bullied, but when they cannot defend themselves, it is just cruel.

One day, Andy was shopping with me at the local store, whose staff knew Andy and were kind to him. When we got outside, boys about his age were on bikes and skateboards and went thundering past us. He was carrying a bag of tomatoes for me. He looked up at me and said, 'I want to do that, mummy.' It broke my heart.

Faith Healing

I had already tried to take Andy to a faith healer in 1985 when I lived in Kent. I would try anything! An American faith healer was appearing at the Chatham Central Hall, so a friend

(Maggie) and I attended. Apparently, the faith-healer was well-known on this circuit as the amount of people attending was staggering.

We managed to elbow our way into the front stalls. Andy was not in the slightest bit concerned about the amount of people present. He carried on making his noises and his high-pitched 'Eeeeeey' sound as the place filled up. The faith healer came on stage and soon realised that there would be no real atmosphere if Andy didn't shut up making his screeches. So, he gestured towards us, looking fairly irritated, saying 'Come up, little man, don't be shy.' Andy was helped onto the stage by huge American minders – with his ribbon and bell on his right arm and his leg splint on his right leg - and stood next to the main man looking very pleased with himself and not at all shy.

Then, the man laid hands on Andy and began to talk in tongues. The place erupted with people who were now also talking in tongues and waving their arms in the air. After the American blessed him and Andy was being helped off stage, we were politely asked to leave by the minders as the noises he was making were 'too much of a distraction'. My friend, Andy and I had to exit out of a side door so as not to reduce the atmosphere even more - which we thought was hilarious. Not very Christian!

Fast forward to Blackpool, 1987. Caroline was friendly with the local vicar's daughter. He and his wife also had four children and were really nice to Andy. One day, they asked me if I would object to them having a laying on of hands ceremony with the objective being to heal Andy. I mentioned that this had actually already been tried but the vicar persuaded me that it was worth a go. Naturally I agreed.

50

The agreed Sunday teatime came, and I arrived at the allotted time. Four more believers were there. They had laid out toys like coloured, wooden bricks and Lego for Andy as they knew that he liked to build towers, as tall as he could make them. That week, Man 2 Man with Man Parrish had been on Top of the Pops, with their hit *Male Stripper*. Andy really loved that record because of the electronic voice on it, which constantly repeated, 'I met a male stripper in a go-go bar.'

The ceremony started with prayers and then the speaking in tongues of the people gathered, who all held hands; myself included, as I'd been asked to, so I couldn't really say no. The holding of hands, not the speaking in tongues. I was reminded of Spike Milligan guesting on a chat show. He'd said something about people speaking in tongues sounding like they were saying, 'Iggery buggery. Iggery buggery.' It sounded just like that. So, I was feeling a little uncertain to say the least. Andy had been playing with the Lego and the wooden bricks very nicely until he began to feel ignored. He started to systematically aim for the backs of the believers' heads with the wooden bricks. He was (and still is) a crack shot. To their credit, they tried to ignore him, even though they must have been hurt. The chanting only increased.

Then, Andy's piece de resistance. He started to mimic the electronic voice of the male stripper record. There was 'Iggery buggery' and 'I met a male stripper in a go-go bar' going simultaneously. I was dying to laugh but really couldn't as they were well-meaning and trying hard to help me and Andy. I made my excuses and left and, as soon as I was out of earshot, laughed all the way home.

Chapter 5

Recompense

The Out-of-Court-Settlement

Steve had always promised that he would get his revenge on Dr Khan for mis-diagnosing Andy's meningitis. The way that he could do this was by trying to ruin Dr Khan's reputation in court and by securing Andy's future by suing the doctor for as much money as he could. This was way before the litigious culture of today. Steve started legal proceedings in late 1981, shortly after he realised that Andy would never get better and that, in his opinion, Dr Khan had effectively ruined Andy's life. This was not an easy process as the medical profession was notoriously tight within itself, and unwelcoming to anyone who wanted information that might put a slur on their good practice.

Knowing his guilt, Dr Khan had tried to lie his way out of culpability. He had even amended his doctor's notes on Andy's records (which took three years to be released) by putting an omission mark under a sentence and adding 'tested for neck stiffness' above it. He actually shot himself in the foot with that addition to the records, because babies of fifteen-month old do not have neck stiffness if they contract meningitis… a worrying omission to add to medical records, considering that any properly qualified doctor should surely have known this fact. By January 1989, the case was ready for High Court.

The Award

By the strong belief that he had a case, and the written efforts of the solicitor, (and some written testimony from me), Steve got the negligence case to court - eight years after Andy had contracted meningitis. The medical profession really did stick together.

In April 1989, Andy was awarded £750,000 – a huge sum of money in 1989. This award was for the rest of Andy's life. It was thought that he would probably have gone to university and had a well-paid job; it was estimated on economic criteria. Now, he would never grow up to realise his potential in the normal world, so his needs were different but still economically high. He would need a house; he would need carers round the clock or a specialist school and adult placement when, or if, the time came that I could no longer cope with him. His lifespan was reckoned by health professionals to be in his thirties. This was based on the damage that his constant epileptic fits were doing and also the fact that he could kill himself in a drop fit.

When the papers got hold of the story, an article was printed in the local paper (absolutely nothing to do with me) and the local paper where we had lived in Kent (definitely a neighbour) giving out the amount and naming our family. Within days, I had lots of begging letters which I placed straight in the bin. Unbelievable! The compensation money was for the rest of Andy's life, not some stranger's gas bill – and it was Andy's money, not mine.

The first thing to be done when the money came through was to move into a larger property where we would all have more space, a key consideration. When a person is volatile and has unpredictable bouts of violence, it is better that they are not crowded in any way and can demand attention when they need it, rather than having it foist upon them. From my, and his siblings, point of view more space was essential to escape should Andy come running at us with intent to harm. This was a daily consideration.

We found the perfect property in Victoria Road East, Thornton: a large, Victorian semi-detached house with three living rooms, a dining room, a large kitchen, five bedrooms and a huge back garden. Four bedrooms really, but one large bedroom had been divided into a bedroom and dressing room – perfect for rooms for me and Andy, as we had to get up so early. This could be done without disturbing any of the others as we were at the opposite side of the house to Caroline, Bobby and Tommy. We moved on the eleventh of April 1989, just days before the Hillsborough disaster.

I really thought that having this indoor and outdoor space would make a positive difference and it did, at first. But Andy was getting bigger, stronger and more aggressive. He was growing up and his developing testosterone levels were getting higher and higher. This did not improve his behaviour and it was by this time that I had serious concerns about how Andy was going to end up. Would he always be totally ungovernable when he lost his temper? How would he cope as an adult if this 'kicking off' did not stop? And, how would we?

Constant Violence

We lived at Victoria Road East for three years and eight months. In that time, the children and I had multiple injuries. When I say injuries, I am not exaggerating. This behaviour was not behaviour that could be ignored. I am not describing slaps, pushes or shouting insults. I am talking about full-force punches, scratches and pinches, head-butts, kicks, shoving with intent to push downstairs, spitting, biting with intent to rip a chunk of flesh out of your arm, stomach, leg – wherever happened to be nearest. Throwing heavy objects with a good aim and intent to hurt. It was full-blown violence.

The behaviour could sometimes be predicted. He would repeat himself to wind himself up, for example, 'I want another catalogue, I want another catalogue, I want another catalogue…' On and on. Often, he would accompany the repetition by banging his fist on the floor or where he was sitting or hit himself, or head butt the window (maximum damage). Meanwhile, his brown eyes would turn black as the pupils dilated and he would take a pot shot at the nearest person, or the person refusing his demands, or take a run at them. It was surprising how fast Andy could move when he was in the grip of this temper.

Or, it was completely unpredictable. There have been many times that we've been having a cuddle that has turned into a head butt (and I have the shattered cheekbone to prove it). Someone, anyone, the nearest person, indoors or outdoors could get hurt without any warning.

So, it was at this time that I had to become Andy's bouncer. When the children had friends around, which was most of the time - or even when they didn't - I would stick to Andy to protect my other children (and other people's children) so that they could all have normal, quality playtime with their friends. I even took Andy with me to the toilet. But now and again, he would slip my grip, attention or book reading to try to attack his siblings or their friends. The injuries were horrendous. I did manage to keep the children's attacks to a minimum by my bouncer role but I had split lips, many a bloodied nose, loosened teeth, was black and blue all over and had scars and scratches all over my hands where he would suddenly nip me.

My hands looked so bad that I was asked by a supermarket check-out girl what had happened. I said that I had two German shepherd dogs - this was true - and that I'd been playing with them. I really could be bothered to tell the truth.

It is fair to say that in the three years and eight months that we were in the house, Andy had transformed from a naughty but amusing boy into a dangerous and far from funny young man. He had also discovered masturbation and would try to do this in public or in front of the children's friends (much to their amusement or embarrassment, depending on their age), even though he knew that it was something that he should do in his room, in private. He liked delivering the maximum upset to people and he loved to be the centre of attention, at any cost. Life was really hard for all of us. Then my sister said one day, 'Why are you being so selfish? What about your other children?' And I knew she was right, but it was just such a hard decision to make. I felt that I was letting Andy down and I felt that I was a real failure as his mum. But Andy wasn't my only child - and my sister really was right.

Andy's Expulsion

By this time (April 1991), Andy had been expelled from Highfurlong School. There were many reasons for this. Not only had his behaviour spiralled out of control, so that even the lovely, patient, 1:1 staff employed to assist Andy had complained and refused to work with him, but he was also banned from the school bus, for the safety of the other children. Andy had a short spell of being picked up and dropped back home by taxi, paid for by the Education Department, but this was doomed. The last taxi driver that dropped Andy back home shouted, 'If he hits me again, or pulls my hair or spits I'm going to hammer him. He's a little bastard!' and in all fairness, I couldn't actually disagree with him. So, I said, 'I'm really sorry, I wish he didn't do that too,' but the taxi driver understandably told me to fuck off. The taxis lasted all of four weeks.

I was so sick and tired of repeatedly apologising for Andy's behaviour - although I still did it - and trying to socialise, calm and 'normalise' him. I was worn-out and tired too; he still only slept about three to four hours at night, and still woke up around three to four in the morning, generally with a punch in the face for me.

Then came the crunch. I received a phone call from the school to come immediately and pick Andy up. Obviously, something awful had happened. I was told just how awful when I got to Highfurlong. A boy in Andy's year with cerebral palsy had recently had a neurosurgical operation for a metal plate to be put in his head. This was meant to stabilise the boy's movements and help him to have some control over them, if possible. He had only just recovered from the operation and returned to school when Andy had an episode of sudden violence and punched the boy with his fist on top of his head.

The boy had to be sent home and then straight to the hospital where everything had to be checked to see if the results of the operation had been reduced by the blow. I was appalled and angry with Andy – but also extremely worried about the health of the injured boy. The next evening, I arranged for my mum to look after everyone whilst I got the address of the boy from Mr. Roberts, the headmaster of Highfurlong.

I found out that the boy was back at home from Mr. Roberts (who I think felt sorry for me). He told me that the boy was recovering and that no major harm was done. I took Andy with me – I now couldn't leave him with my mum and the other children - and locked him in the car whilst I went to see the parents. Andy booted the windows and punched the windscreen whilst I waited at the door.

The parents opened the door, waited to hear what I had to say, then told me that they didn't particularly blame me, but could I not instil right and wrong upon my child? I tried to explain the circumstances but understandably, they weren't interested. They basically told me that if they ever saw Andy anywhere near their boy, they would do the same to him. They asked me to never come near their home again and that they were requesting that Andy was expelled. Then, they slammed the door in my face. I looked at Andy in the car banging and punching away and my heart sank.

Chapter 6

A New Approach

Almost Beechtree School

It was clear to me that we were at the end of the road. All my attempts to make Andy 'normal' had failed. He was psychopathic in his behaviours. He didn't care one iota if he really hurt someone. They weren't important to him. All that WAS important were HIS needs and HIS wants and if he didn't get the objects of his needs and wants, he intimidated, bullied and injured people until he did. (We used to liken him to Spoilt Bastard in the adult comic Viz). Violence was the only power that he had in his life as he needed round the clock support in all other areas. I understood this but it didn't make for a carefree life for my children or me. He was still my son and I loved him, but this could not be allowed to go on.

I did what was necessary to get an interview for Beechtree School and made my first visit a month after Andy was expelled. It was clear that Andy's case was a critical one or the miles of red tape would have taken much longer to shift. I was shown around the downstairs of the building by the head before we went to her office. In the entrance hallway of the school, some of the parquet flooring had been taken up, so I said by way of conversation, 'Are you decorating?' and the answer was, 'No, not really. One of our young men chewed that part of the floor, so we're replacing it.' I was not shocked by this answer. In fact, I thought this was a positive. They weren't going to be shocked by Andy's behaviour!

After many assessments, meetings and talks by health professionals, it was decided that Andy should start in early September of 1991. In some ways, this could not come quickly enough for me and the kids. In others, I felt guilty, a failure, imagined Andy being unhappy staying in a strange place, imagined him missing his family and wanting his mum. I can't describe how bad I felt about the whole situation. I kept wishing that things would change for the better, that he'd never had meningitis or that he'd have died instead of living – the guilt went on and on. I didn't sleep at all and in the daytime, I was punched, kicked and spat at.

It was a hot July. I was exhausted, depressed and worried. Andy, Bobby and Tommy were asleep, and Caroline was staying at her friend's house for the night. I decided that I couldn't let Andy go to Beechtree School. How would he cope without us? I couldn't give up on him like that. I made the decision that I would have to kill him instead.

Andy and I slept at the other side of the house, so Bobby and Tommy wouldn't hear anything, I thought. I crept upstairs with three carrier bags put together with the intent of suffocating Andy as he slept. I would wait until he was no longer breathing, then remove the bags and destroy them in random supermarket bins. That was my plan. I got as far as putting the bags over his forehead. Andy awoke and said, 'Don't do that, mummy.' I burst into tears and cuddled him, saying 'Sorry Andy, sorry Andy', over and over.

I couldn't believe I'd gone this far. I knew that I was potentially having some sort of breakdown. I hadn't slept for nearly twelve years. I'd had chicken pox which had turned into shingles. I had permanent diarrhoea and sickness. I had psoriasis covering my head and body (it was even in the whites of my eyes) like Dennis Potter's 'Singing Detective' and I weighed under seven stone. If Andy stayed at home, I knew that I would die, then what would happen to all of my children? I was positive then that Andy was going to attend Beechtree School when the time came, and who knows, he might even like it?

Beechtree School

I cannot fault the staff at Beechtree School for their commitment, their good will and their inability to be shocked by random, violent, sexual behaviours and even riper language that came from some of the pupils - but mainly from Andy. The staff were young, well-trained, had a good sense of humour and believed in – as I did - inclusion for their pupils.

At first, I was encouraged to agree not to visit Andy for the first month so that he could get into some sort of routine with the staff, and for him not to come home at the weekends during this time. He eventually came home every other weekend whilst we were still at Victoria Road East. This was a difficult time. Andy was very angry at us all – understandably – and I felt a huge amount of guilt. I'd enjoyed the peace and quiet with no constant shouting, swearing or violence – and so had the children. He must have felt really rejected and I felt awful about that. We carried on and persisted with every other weekend though and tried very hard to make him happy, most of the time unsuccessfully.

However, because of Andy's change of circumstances, the Court of Protection decided that the family should probably move to a smaller house, as the chances of Andy living in a home environment permanently again were very slim. I found a house that was ideal for us – another Victorian terrace – this time, next to a field and a short walk to the beach. It was down the road for the other kids' schools too. Perfect. When we moved, on the fourth of December 1992, it was near Christmas – traditionally a very stimulating time for Andy. His birthday and Christmas were not a good time for Andy. He could not cope with the lead up to Christmas, his anticipation mirrored in the media by way of toy adverts, happy family gatherings and tins of favourite chocolates every day for weeks, then the day itself. Christmas Day became a massive anti-climax for him and by afternoon, he was having a violent outburst of one kind or another.

The New House

Andy came home for that first Christmas at our new address at 61, Fleetwood Road. The visit was a few days before Christmas (optimistic of me) and it was a real failure. I picked him up from Beechtree and put his seat belt on. He was on the back seat of a seven-seater people carrier and I was driving, so I thought, there was enough space for the drive from Preston to Blackpool to be safe. He was effectively banked in by the middle seats, or so I thought. We had only been in the car for about fifteen minutes when I noticed that Andy had taken off his seat belt and was coming towards me at speed with his 'good' hand outstretched.

I had long hair in a ponytail, and, from experience, I knew what the next step would be. We were on the motorway doing about eighty miles-per-hour so that I could get home as quickly as possible – and it was then that Andy grabbed my hair and yanked my head back so that I couldn't see the road. I had to pull up on the hard shoulder and bribe Andy to be 'good'. 'Didn't he want any Christmas presents, didn't he want to see his new bedroom, didn't he want to see his sister and brothers?' Eventually, he calmed down and we made it home - but I knew that his mood hadn't gone away.

Not only was it a new environment for Andy to come to but the house was much smaller than Victoria Road East and therefore, more dangerous, if he was to have an episode of hyper-violence which, of course, he did. It started after about half an hour with Andy trying to smash a window, then an attempt to attack his siblings at random downstairs, then an attempt to break the television – a complete nightmare for the children and me. I managed to get Andy to come upstairs with me, but he showed no sign of calming down at all. He spat at me and tried to bite me. At thirteen-years-old, he was bigger than me and very powerful. The only thing I could do was to keep him in the bedroom by holding the door shut on the outside while Caroline called Beechtree to come and pick him up. There was no chance of him being able to stay.

After half an hour of pure mayhem, the staff from Beechtree arrived. The kids and I got out of the way so that the staff could get him downstairs without hitting us. The staff were really good. They told us not to worry and that this was quite a common reaction, what with it being Christmas and a new environment. So back to Beechtree Andy went, taking his presents with him.

I decided after that visit that I could never put the children – or myself – through that experience again. For the first time I'd actually been frightened of my own son and the kids, especially Tommy, had been terrified. I decided that I would visit him twice a week at Beechtree and the kids could visit if or when they wanted to.

Womaston School, Powys

The feeder school for Beechtree was Womaston School in mid-Wales. At that time, it was the most appropriate school that disabled children were placed in, not the nearest in their area, so it was decided after many meetings, that Womaston was the most appropriate placement. I went to visit Womaston with two workers from Beechtree who I got on well with. We all decided that it seemed like a really good place. It was in the deep countryside with the Brecon Beacons in the distance so Andy could have lots of freedom as Womaston was enclosed on a very large plot of land. It was a large manor-like house with two separate buildings for bedrooms.

There was a bus for trips out into Hereford to pursue interests like shopping or swimming or bowling, so it wasn't as if Andy would be locked away. They had a good arts and crafts room and schoolroom. The food seemed really good and the staff were really positive. It seemed perfect for him.

I decided that it was the best place for Andy until it was time for him to go to an adult placement – we all agreed on that. I would visit him, work permitting, once a week or once a fortnight. Andy left Beechtree School and attended Womaston School in September 1993. And, again, I was told not to visit for the first fortnight so that he could settle in. I did as I was told and contacted Andy by phone to see if all was going well. I spoke to the staff there too, so that I had some contact with what was happening in Andy's life. He seemed a long way away and that was pretty worrying.

Andy seemed to thrive for the first two years of being there. He went on holiday to London to see his father with three staff and that was a success. He went camping with his staff locally, in Herefordshire. He came to Blackpool for a week with three staff and that also was a success. Then, because he was getting so big, he was moved into the bigger boy's house in the Womaston grounds. Any change in routine always brought about a negative change in Andy's behaviours, so I expected the worst.

The Big Boys House

Andy's first placement at Womaston was only next door to the Big Boys House which was to be his second placement there. He was getting older and bigger, so it was the custom for the children to move on. There was not a great deal of change environmentally. Of course, he had a new room, so that was different, as were the other pupils. More importantly though, the staff were different - and he knew (Andy could understand a lot more than people gave him credit for) - that this was the last stop before his foray into the world of adult placement which was beginning to be a worry for him.

In the two years that Andy was in the Big Boys House, his behaviour deteriorated rapidly. His behaviour was appalling at times before this, but there would be periods of happiness and laughter. Not anymore. He was now fifteen and would constantly masturbate in his room (and out of it, for maximum effect). His behaviour became more and more dangerous and violent. I would make the drive to see him from Blackpool to Womaston every week or two weeks, depending on my work.

I had to start off at 4.30a.m. so that I could get there for 8.30a.m. at the latest. By 8.30a.m., he would have had his breakfast and would be ready to see me – rather like royalty or a waiting statesman. He was always at the window looking out for me by the time I arrived, and I could usually tell if he was pleased or angry by the look on his face.

If he was pleased and happy to see me, we would have a good visit. We would maybe have a walk round the grounds alone, throw stones in the stream when it was summer, go to the art room in winter and see his creations or make some of our own.

However, if his expression was blank and unmoving, I knew that it was going to be bad. And it was often bad. I could be kicked, punched, bitten, sworn at, spat at or have things thrown at me. If this happened, the staff would rush in and physically restrain him. (Acceptable behaviour at the time). I would say, 'Right Andy, I have to go now', and he would be screaming 'Mummy don't go, don't go….I'm calm now, I'm calm now'...which of course, he wasn't. His eyes would be black and glazed and he wanted the staff to let him go so that he could have another pop at me.

I would have to drive home with 'Mummy, don't go, don't go,' ringing in my ears, make tea for everyone, make sure the boys did their homework and went to bed, make sure Caroline and her best friend Amanda were home to babysit, (I paid them) then do a waking watch starting at 10 p.m. for Liverpool and Lancashire Autistic Society (now Autism Initiatives). Fortunately, the house I worked in was only a few yards from where I lived. I wouldn't have slept that night anyway.

In the last year that Andy was in the Big Boys House, all his behaviour logs and day-to-day happenings were being sent on to appropriate adult placements. Because of the deterioration in his behaviour, none were very keen to take him on. I'd already visited two placements in the South of England, which I'd really liked, but over time, they decided that he would be too much for them. There was one left and I was going to have a look at it. It was also in the Powys area, so I thought that this might have been good for Andy as it would be a continuity of sorts - and I was really hoping that I would get a good vibe from it. Unfortunately, circumstances dictated that I would never visit this placement.

Andy and

GOOD BYE.
& Goodbye
Star of the Show!

PUMA
MR. UPPITY
LITTLE MISS SHY
LITTLE MISS SPLENDID
LITTLE MISS DOTTY

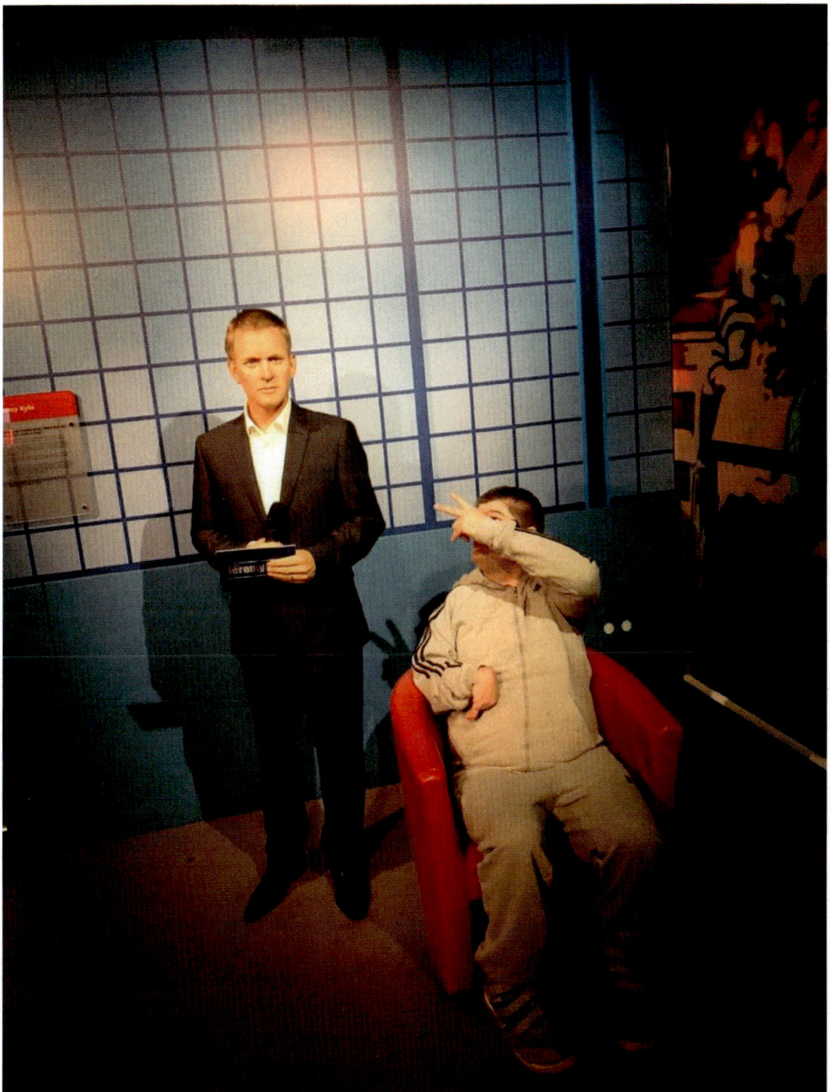

PUMA

Chapter 7

Bereavement

The Call
I was now working for Social Services in a scheme called the Core and Cluster. This was an arrangement where the main offices were near the various houses where people lived who needed support with everyday life. They usually had varying degrees of intellectual disability, sometimes physical disability and sometimes mental health problems. It was well known that I had an extremely violent, intellectually and physically disabled son, so I usually got sent to jobs that perhaps other staff members might have objected to. (In fact, one doctor had described Andy as the most challenging boy in Lancashire, so my job future was sewn up).

My shift time was between six to nine in the evening. I was at a job at about seven o'clock on the fourth of August 1997, when I received a call from the Head Office saying that my sister-in-law was on the phone. This surprised me because since divorcing Andy's dad, Steve, we hadn't spoken at all. I answered the call from Avril, Steve's sister, who just about was able to tell me, between sobs, that there'd been an accident and that Steve had been run over by a black cab on Holloway Road in London. He had died in the ambulance on the way to hospital.

I was completely shocked. I asked if I could go home as I needed to see my children to tell them. They kindly let me go. Caroline was getting ready for a night out – a twenty-first - and said that she couldn't think about it now but would come home later, then address it. She was totally in shock. Bobby was in America, on holiday with his then girlfriend Jodie and her family, so I made the decision not to tell him until he came back in two days' time. Tommy had gone to a friend's house and was due home at nine o'clock, so I waited until I could stand it no longer and went to look for him and saw him as he was walking home. It was a terrible time for all of the children.

Caroline insisted on telling Andy herself the day after and drove down to Womaston. Afterwards, she thought that, although Andy had taken it in and knew that his dad was now in heaven (the only way to explain it to Andy), he didn't really get it. Let's be honest, it's bad enough when you haven't got a learning disability to take in the enormity of never seeing a loved one again. Of course, this meant trouble for and with Andy. Steve had visited Womaston about once a month, so Andy had received regular contact with him. A regular point of excitement and treats had gone, as had the company of a dad that he loved.

The deterioration after August 1997 was remarkable in its intensity. The staff admitted that they had lost control of Andy and also admitted to increasing his dose of anti-psychotic medication, under doctor's orders. Let me say now that when your child goes into care, which residential schools are in effect, then you have no say in decisions like the upping of medication. When he had lived at home, he had no medication at all after I found that the Epilim and Tegretol didn't work - but since Beechtree School and then Womaston School, he was on a host of anti-psychotics and mood stabilisers – that also clearly did not work and had the side effect of making him angry and depressed.

He was 'kicking off' all the time at Womaston and the number of staff needed to restrain him was getting larger, as I found out when I asked to look at his daily logs, and was shocked to find that at least three people were used in these restraints. I mentioned to the staff that I thought these were heavy handed tactics that clearly didn't work, but they felt that they had no alternative as his medication had also been increased, also with no effect.

I expect it's called 'grief'(!) but being Andy, and with everyone becoming frightened of him, they decided that counselling was clearly out of the question.

Sectioning and Expulsion

Andy's birthday is on the thirtieth of October. In 1997, he was making the staff's life a complete misery by wanting his birthday NOW. His behaviours were getting to danger level according to the staff, so I decided to visit, as usual, on a Monday, three days before his actual birthday for his birthday brought forward, with his chocolates and presents. When I got there, I can only describe Andy as being in a drug induced coma. I was appalled as I'd been travelling since four-thirty in the morning to get to see him. The staff apologised profusely – and embarrassedly - and said that they feared for my safety as he'd been so violent. I blew up. I said words to the effect of 'Don't you think I know what he's capable of? I'd rather be punched than see him like this, on whose authority did you give him the overdose? Are you trying to kill him?' I went on and on.

This wasn't particularly fair of me, as hadn't I sent him there with my blessing because I could no longer cope? Also, most of the staff were really good and Andy loved them. But, in my defence, the sight of Andy lying comatose on his bed was shocking and very unsettling. I stayed my usual length of time (four hours) whilst Andy flitted in and out of consciousness, then I left, totally disgusted and very worried about what was going on in that space. I visited every week after this incident and phoned to see that he was still around. I phoned the staff that I had bonded with – and trusted - every day. I got a litany of horror stories about Andy being restrained regularly from those trusted members of staff, and stories of Andy crying in his room - not like Andy at all. Andy was quite unemotional unless it was anything to do with his collections, or something being taken off him that he wanted. Then and only then would he show any emotion. This was all very upsetting - especially when Andy was miles away and I had three other children and a job to contend with.

I usually visited Andy on a Monday, as I did on the twenty-fourth of November 1997. Andy was not at his window. I was called immediately into the headmaster's room. He announced that the last available adult placement had refused Andy on the grounds that he had had a restraint involving five members of staff and the placement felt that they did not have the resources to be able to support him. I said 'Sorry, hang on, did you say five members of staff?' I worked with people who had extremely challenging behaviours and I'd never heard of anything like this. I asked if the staff involved had had any restraint training and I was told, 'Yes'. So, I asked, 'So why did you need five people?' He did not have a sufficiently coherent answer. And that's when he dropped his bombshell.

'We believe that Andy should be sectioned under the Mental Health Act of 1983 as he can no longer cope with being here and we can no longer cope with his behaviours.' In effect, they were expelling him and sectioning him. Sectioning! So, I asked the Head when he thought he was going to do this, and he said in one week's time. The abridged version of my answer is, 'Oh no you're not, sunshine.' I persuaded the head that I would look after my son and I would start a placement with just him and that I could find adequate, TRAINED staff with no problem; so don't even think of sectioning Andy, as it would be over his (the head's) own dead body. I arranged then and there with the head that Andy should be sent back to area to an address that I would inform him of in a couple of days' time. Then I went and had my mum visit with my semi-conscious son.

One Week to Find a Placement

I returned to Blackpool in a daze. I knew that time was extremely limited and that I had to make a list of all the people that I knew that could actually, physically help me.

I phoned the Court of Protection where Andy's money was held, and I asked the Receiver if she could advise me. I told her the potential situation and that I would do anything to stop Andy being sectioned. He'd had meningitis for God's sake! This deterioration wasn't his fault, it was part of his condition: also, there were the possibility that some staff were untrained in challenging behaviour techniques, his raised testosterone levels, the unlimited use of anti-psychotic medication which causes depression and his fear of an adult placement - which had been, stupidly, openly discussed in front of him.

I got in touch with the Court of Protection lady who ran Andy's account as his Receiver, Pam and told her what had happened and what I wanted to do. Eventually, I wanted to buy a house for Andy with his own money, but I only had a week to get a roof over his head! He clearly could not live at home. I needed some of Andy's money released - so that I could rent a property for six months whilst this was in hand, as the ideal property had to be found. I also needed to pay the staff that I would cobble together. Andy would need at least two to three staff on a twenty-four hours basis for at least six months, as the trauma of change would completely unsettle him – his violence would be off the scale.

I knew with working for Social Services that when it came to a large funding package, they would drag their feet for as long as possible. We worked out that Andy would have to pay for his own staff until we could some to some sort of arrangement with the Health Authority and Social Services. This would take some time. We worked out that I would have to be up-front with potential landlords as real damage could be done to their investments. We calculated six months' rent (at the time about £4-500 per month for a house or apartment and approximately £2,500 per week for Andy's staffing (three staff at twenty-four hours per day and two sleepovers). Considering that the next months would be tough to say the least, this was all a necessity, not an extravagance.

All of the requests were agreed. Then the hunt for the house or flat was on. Bobby gave up his college course to work hands-on and Caroline gave up her job for the administrative side of the operation. Tommy was still at school. I knew someone from Social Services who was looking for a new challenge (Nikky), I knew my nephew who lived in Lancaster needed a job - and had always got on with – and understood - Andy. A friend of my nephew who had care experience wanted to work with us and that was it! We only had another five days to go. Meanwhile, a house to rent had been found but it was far from perfect. It was a tiny two-up, two-down in nearby Cleveleys – but the landlord was going to renovate after the six months, so he wasn't too bothered about a mess. Obviously, it depended on how big a mess, but he was pretty good about the situation.

An advert went in the paper for more staff, second-hand furniture was bought; we all got together for discussions about continuity and where to get training for possible restraints and how to avoid them. We needed to know more about the new positive behavioural support (this was 1997) that was being lauded in care - we wanted to do the job properly. D-Day (or A-Day) was the first of December 1997 and we were expecting Andy around twelve noon.

Chapter 8

Andy's Own Placement

Return to Area

The day came for his return, the first of December 1997. Andy and his support staff from Womaston arrived, as expected, at twelve noon, in a white van packed with his belongings. The outreach team from Womaston consisted of four interchangeable staff members who had got on pretty well with Andy. They had told Andy that very same morning that – 'guess what Andy? You're going to get your own key to a house back in the Blackpool area! You'll be near your family!'

I understand why they did that. This was because, if the move had been spoken about at the beginning of the week, Andy would have been dangerously aroused, worried and frightened - and would have probably been sedated because of his behaviours, so they did the right thing, in a way.

Andy was quiet and a little disorientated – naturally – and his staff were being positive and cheerful to try to liven him up. We were all welcoming him and also being positive and smiley, something that was important to Andy. He liked it when people were pleased to see him, as we all do; not scared or pissed off that he was there.

We decided that it was time to have something to eat, then we would unpack his clothes and belongings. This went well. We got some fish and chips, which Andy loved, then we showed him his bedroom, with the other bedroom next to it for the sleep-over staff. We came downstairs to find the outreach staff bringing in boxes and boxes of smelly, old Kentucky Fried Chicken boxes (containing the bones), countless plastic containers crammed with marshmallow sweets called Flumps and his collection of Mr. Men books, Little Miss books and frayed looking catalogues. I had expected those. After all, when I went to visit him, I always brought two Mr. Men books with me. I also brought him a Christmas catalogue when they came in the shops - but masses of rotting bones and squashed up sweets?

I asked the staff why they had brought them, and they said that they hadn't dared to take them off Andy because he might have been really angry. They wanted his transition to go as smoothly as possible and didn't want to upset him. Clearly, the roles had become confused as to who was the enabled and who was the enabler. When I asked why the boxes of bones and the mouldy sweets had become a collection in the first place, they did not have a satisfactory answer. I expect they were so sick of the violence that they had let him do exactly what he wanted for a quiet life. I could understand this blind-eye approach, but from experience - and not just with Andy - this is the very thing that should NOT be done if a set of challenging behaviours are to be modified.

The outreach staff were staying in a hotel nearby - paid for by Andy - so when they had gone, we decided to get rid of the smelly, rotten boxes of bones. I said 'Andy, you don't really want these do you? You can't eat the sweets and there's nothing left of the Kentucky but smelly bones! Ugh! He agreed almost instantly.

Andy laughed whilst we threw the rubbish into the boot of my car, ready to take to the tip the next day. My theory is that the only area of life that Andy had any control over was his ability to receive fear from others by his violent behaviour. So, he'd been exerting his power for his own recovery of equality, I suppose, after the body blows of the death of his father and the excessive use of medication by the staff, which acted as a restraint on his behaviours. And now, he would have to deal with the area move. This had all been dictated to him by his staff at Womaston and was totally out of his control. These crucial decisions were being made for him, without any previous open discussion with him, by others. No wonder he was angry.

An Unsuitable Home

The house that we had rented for Andy between December 1997 and April 1998 just did not work. It was a tiny two up, two down. The smallness of it was nearly lethal - but we'd had no choice. There was a front room and tiny kitchen with just enough room for a small table and two chairs. Then, there were some very steep stairs leading to two small bedrooms, one for a staff member and one for Andy. At this time, two members of staff would be with Andy until he fell asleep (about 10p.m.) then one staff member would go home to return at 7a.m. It was fingers crossed that Andy didn't wake up during the night. We just didn't have enough staff to cover two sleeps at night-time in these early days, but we were trying to interview as many potential staff as possible so as to find more (people willing to get beaten up). Not an easy task.

Andy had come back to area with a cocktail of anti-psychotic medication which made him depressed and angry. After we'd got rid of his rancid collections, we concentrated on his 'proper' collections, his Mr. Men and Little Miss Books. We encouraged Andy to care for this collection and possibly add to it. He also like to collect chocolate tubs like the ones to be had at Christmas - Roses chocolate tins, Cadbury's Milk Tray chocolates boxes and Quality Street tins. He was still into his catalogue collection and, as it was Christmas time with all the decorations in the shops, he was very keen to get more. The Argos catalogue was popular, as was Littlewoods and the big stores ones.

Cleveleys was down the road. A small town with all the relevant shops. It had an Argos. At this early stage, we had to use our own cars rather than the bigger people carrier that would be bought later. One person to drive, the other to sit next to Andy in the back seat. In a normal sized car, this was really dangerous. Either the person next to Andy would be attacked, or the driver's hair was pulled so that they couldn't see what was coming towards them on the road. (The other staff and I had personal experience of this many times).

The Argos catalogue was picked up. Andy was very unsettled going into the shops, as they were packed, and demanded a Roses chocolate tub and Milk Tray chocolates at the top of his considerable voice, which were denied – this was for Christmas Day, we had told him. We had to be consistent in our behaviours with him, or the whole care package would fall apart, just has it had done at Womaston School. And these were such early days.

When he got his Argos catalogue back home, he systematically started to rip out the pages, making his collection bigger (i.e. more) and fuelling his obsession. The obsession with more did not always make him happy. It did to an extent, where he would look after his collection and keep it tidy, then, for no apparent reason, the collection began to get on his nerves – it was too big. And who had made it big by his demands? And his ripping of pages to make the collection bigger? Yes, Andy himself. He would deliberately work himself up into a rage, saying that he couldn't find a particular page. He would bang on the floor, spit, attack and hurt people.

In fact, what he HAD done was to deliberately hide the page he was supposedly looking for, by pushing it under the couch or under a carpet, so that he could work himself up into a frenzy, the end result being injuries to the staff. This had never happened before in all Andy's obsessional behaviours, so until we realised what was happening, we were searching for a scrap of torn paper that Andy had insisted was lost, just so we didn't get hurt. (Rather like the Womaston staff and the rancid collections!) Fortunately, we did manage to recognise what he was doing when we found the missing bit of paper where he had put it. We then put in place strategies of how to deal in a consistent way with this behaviour.

We also noticed that, although Andy had always sworn, he displayed overtly sexual behaviour. He constantly masturbated, he would try to grab people's bodies and his language was overtly sexual, which it had never been before. One of his favourites was, 'I'm going to put a big fat willy in your gob.' The first time it was said, I asked him to repeat it, as I thought that I had mis-heard. It was pretty shocking. Here was a young man of just gone eighteen with profound learning disabilities who was deliberately making himself unhappy and speaking in a way that we'd never heard before. I put it down to the former staff speaking out of turn and the medication at the time.

Christmas Build-up

From the 1st December to the 25th December 1997, there had been multiple injuries to staff. My nephew Paul's friend, also called Paul had done the sleep-over and I was coming in to relieve him at 7a.m. When he opened the door, I was shocked to see the state of his lower lip. It was literally split halfway down to his chin and needed stitches badly. Then there was my kiss that turned into a head-butt and shattered my cheek bone (this would happen again), Bobby's black-eye's and bruises, Caroline's bruises from punches and kicks, the same with Nikky and the same with both Pauls. We needed some extra help. Although we had advertised and gained new staff, they didn't last very long – possibly one of two shifts – then they would leave, never to return.

Christmas was fast approaching. We had approached another care company in the Lancashire area to lend us some staff as we knew that Christmas would be pretty rough. Even so, Caroline had to be on with one of the managers of the other care company on Christmas Day; two women and one Andy, not a great combination. I had been working non-stop since Andy came back to area, Bobby had done multiple shifts, so Caroline said that she'd work on the day. I wasn't very happy about this, but I had my mother coming for Christmas Day, two sons at home and the man that I went on to marry, Eamon, already living with us. I arranged for Caroline to come around for Christmas dinner with the other care worker and, of course, bring Andy.

The time came. Caroline, the female agency care worker and Andy arrived, and all went well for about thirty minutes. Everyone was trying to make Andy feel really welcome – even Tommy, who was really wary of him. (This was because Andy used to target Tommy whenever my back was turned. Andy was aware that he was a big lad and that Tommy was the youngest, not yet as tall as Andy, so it was total bullying).

Andy suddenly followed me into the kitchen and within seconds had hold of my hair and was banging my head against a cupboard door whilst kicking me. Eamon managed to get Andy off me and got him onto the nearest couch where he restrained him for an hour and a half. All the while, Andy was repeating, 'I'm calm now, I'm calm now, I'm calm now,' with the familiar glazed, black eyes in place. Clearly, he was not, and he was getting more and more angry. Eamon, no slouch to physical restraint as a boxer and ex-bouncer, was beginning to get tired and very sweaty. His hands kept slipping off Andy and every time they did, Andy would land a punch. In one instance, Andy managed to boot one of the room-dividing doors in, until Eamon got hold of him again. It was clear that we had no alternative but to call the police and get him to a hospital.

After Christmas 1997

The police were called. They could see the devastation that Andy had caused, both in property and people. They restrained him, hand-cuffed him (difficult and painful because of his hemiplegia) and took him in a Black Maria to the local hospital's psychiatric ward, which was Ward 30 at that time. The police had no training in mental health then and so treated Andy as they would have done any young thug. This was to be expected. Eamon, Caroline and I followed the van. The boys stayed with Grandma at my house. Andy was met by hospital staff as the police had called ahead of our arrival.

We stayed with Andy whilst he was sedated, and the staff arranged a bed for him. Meanwhile, we had to arrange for our staff to be with Andy, as there was absolutely no way that the hospital staff would have been able to cope with him and their other patients. Two staff at all times would have to be at the hospital.

The day after, Caroline and I went to the hospital where we met a member of a Social Services department called the Additional Support Team. They had been contacted through the hospital to advise us. Andy was put on a Section 2, under the Mental Health Act (1983). This meant that he could be at the hospital anytime between seventy-two hours and twenty-eight days. Caz and I were desperate to get him out as soon as possible, so we were glad to accept the Additional Support Group's help. At this time, Andy was still paying for the staff and he would have to pay for the Additional Support Team's staff too. That was fine, we thought. They offered us training in restraint techniques, psychologies of behaviour and all the courses that they had. This seemed really helpful - and it would ensure that Andy could come out of hospital after seventy-two hours. They said that they would lease some of their staff to us as and when needed. We really only wanted to get Andy out of the psychiatric ward.

To cut an extremely long story short, their involvement was a double-edged sword. On the one hand, we got him out of hospital. On the other hand, we were not taken seriously as care staff because of the involvement of family members. Even though I had been on lots of courses with The Liverpool and Lancashire Autistic Society (now Autism Initiatives) and Blackpool Social Services, where I'd worked when Andy was at Womaston, I was still 'mum'. It didn't matter how many times we told them that this was an emergency set up and that we were constantly advertising for trained staff. (Many trained, experienced staff lasted half a shift because of Andy's intimidation and some half an hour), they carried on treating us as amateurs.

We endured one of their teams' cod-psychology training (Nikky had a psychology degree) and another member's restraint training - until both Pauls pointed out that the trainer was supposing that the person displaying challenging behaviour was able-bodied and not hemiplegic. Andy's left side was powerful, accurate and lethal but his right side had adapted to his disabilities. With the lack of 'normal' movement of the right side of Andy's body, other parts would take over the violence in an attack.

For example, the use of his right elbow was powerful with a good aim, his head was good at butting, his teeth were accurate even in the event of a messy attack and he had the ability to projectile vomit at will. So, when the trainer had no answer for this, one of the two Pauls pretended to be Andy and the trainer had to restrain him. This sounds like we weren't taking the session seriously, but we really were – all of us having been injured by Andy. The trainer found it difficult.

Rookwood Avenue

The house on Rookwood Avenue that we used between January and April 1998 was a tiny, two bedroomed terrace with no room to escape violent attacks when needed, which was most of the time. It was a disaster. We rented it out for six months because we thought that by this time, the Court of Protection – notoriously slow in those days at releasing monies – would have released the money for a house purchase. Andy should have his own house. He had the money it would make his place in society more secure (so we thought) and it was necessary for his security.

Caroline had stopped working hands-on as she was tired of the injuries that she was receiving. This was totally understandable. She took care of the paperwork and wages whilst Bobby and I still worked hands-on. Bobby had given up any ideas of college at this time so that he could help his brother, which I appreciated very much because of the stability of the staff team. He took many, many beatings and real injuries on my account - and came straight to work when there was an emergency. He was just seventeen years old.

Staff came and went on a regular basis but Nikky also stayed on, thankfully. Nephew Paul and his friend, the other Paul, also stayed. At this particular time, only the five of us were constant members of staff. We needed two staff members to go out into the community with Andy for the safety of the general public – and even then, this may not be enough – so we were working around the clock, especially me, Bobby and Nikky.

Andy's behaviour was not improving. There were good days, but not many. He was violent first thing in the morning until he eventually went to sleep. Andy often used his dad's death as an excuse for hitting staff. It would begin with him saying 'My dad's got dead. My dad's got dead,' over and over. He was also depressed. Andy rarely cried but he would suddenly burst into tears. This was totally out of character for him. His sexual behaviour was as open as when he came back to area. Sexual references were spoken or shouted, he tried to grab people in a sexual way and masturbated constantly, even when he was out in the people carrier and sat next to a member of staff (maximum damage).

He was also on a cocktail of drugs – mainly anti-psychotic ones that, according to the leaflet, could leave the person depressed. No shit. We had enrolled Andy on a doctor's list in the area, but so far there was no need to make an appointment for a common cold. What we needed was an overhaul of the medication and to question the necessity of some of the tablets he was taking.

There were many, many restraints and many staff injuries. Broken fingers, punches, bites, broken noses, black eyes and being spat at were all in a day's work. Sometimes restraints took place in the public sphere and sometimes the police were called because it looked like two people had jumped a disabled young man. The situation was critical. After a particularly bad (horrific – biting, pinching, full-blown head-butts and punching) double shift with Bobby and Nikky, we decided to take him to hospital, where he was sectioned on the tenth of April 1998, Good Friday. This time for three months.

This meant that Andy would officially be on a Section 3:117 of the Mental Health Act and that there would now be time to arrange for a house to be bought for Andy - his own house for his security - and hopefully a deep medication review. A change of the chemical imbalance he was experiencing was urgently needed, as his cocktail of tablets were clearly negatively affecting his behaviour and his moods.

The 'Psychy' Ward

This was how Ward 30 at Victoria Hospital was known locally. We arranged to stay with Andy on a two (staff) to one (Andy) ratio for twenty-four hours a day. This was necessary. Although the individuals that were patients in the ward had psychiatric needs, Andy just didn't fit into their norm. His profound learning disabilities and tendency to random attacks of violence on the nearest person meant that we HAD to have a twenty-four-hour staff presence, 2:1 morning and night. Otherwise, Andy would have been heavily sedated out of necessity and a medication review would have been pointless.

It was here that we met the hospital staff, some of whom would become Andy's staff on his release. The big draw was that I would pay cash in hand and would leave it to them to pay their own Employment Tax. (Hmm.) We poached four members of the hospital staff who got on with Andy and who he liked, too. They were battle-weary with the clientele they dealt with on a daily basis, so they weren't particularly shocked by his behaviours, more like interested, as they'd never really encountered anyone like him before.

The three months on Ward 30 passed and these included some really bad times. At one stage, Andy was given an injection of Acuphase (a drug usually used on patients in the ward with psychotic behaviours) which was supposed to knock him out for at least twenty-four hours. The staff that were with Andy at the time phoned me and told me to get to Ward 30 as soon as possible. When I got there, Andy was in a sound-proofed room with wired windows and was locked in. He showed no sign of being sleepy or calm and was shouting for me. I could tell by his face that he was angry, but more scared. I asked the hospital staff what had happened and as I had expected, Andy had displayed his usual random but intense violence and they felt that they had no alternative but to 'relax' him – even though his own staff were there.

I understood that they did not want an out-of-control situation on their hands, but it was upsetting to see Andy like this. I asked the doctor if I could go in the time-out room with him and they looked at me as if I needed treatment too. I eventually got in there and consoled Andy. Even the psychiatric ward was sick of him!

Chapter 9

Another Devastating Call

A Perfect Bungalow
Whilst Andy was in hospital being supported mainly by staff including myself and Bobby, Caroline took up the challenge of finding a house suitable for someone with Andy's needs. That is, detached, with land front and back, understanding neighbours and large rooms for him – and for his staff - to be able to manoeveur in. She found the perfect bungalow in Stanah, near to where we had lived in Thornton nine years ago. The estate agent had told Caroline that the only downside to the property were the nearness of the electric pylons, which, he was led to believe 'had an adverse effect of people's mental health.' Caroline had answered straight-faced that this wouldn't be a problem. I applied to the Court of Protection for a release of funds for the property. They had been kept up to date with the situation so eventually, we received the funding.

Andy also needed his own seven-seater transport for safety's sake. Seven seats were necessary so that there was room for the staff to have a middle space of seats between themselves and Andy. Then, a much-needed secure staff team was essential who would all have the same answers to his questions and not be intimidated. We agreed that the boundaries imposed upon Andy would have to be fairly rigid. This was necessary for him to feel secure. He had been able to intimidate and bully staff through the fear of violence (very real) and had lost the feeling of safety and security by getting his own way. We would construct a timetable of liked activities, like picnics, shopping, meals out, walks and the beach and stick to it until we noticed any changes in his behaviour. Then we could review what was working and, more importantly, what wasn't.

Andy's release date after the medication review was the third of July 1998 and everything was in place for him to come out of hospital safely. The staff were in place, the rotas were covered, and we were all looking forward to making it work – and confounding Social Services!

At this time, we had the rotas doing a 2:1 ratio of staff to Andy – day and night – as he was so volatile and dangerous. He couldn't quite believe that he had his own house and that he wasn't going to go back to the hospital, where he'd been very unhappy. He'd had his own room when he was on Ward 30, but none of his collections whilst in the ward. So, he'd decided to make a collection of his own toenails by tearing them off and making his feet an agonising, bloody mess. This is how important his collections were to him. He loved them obsessively, but he also didn't really like them very much – a bit like a doomed love affair. He was prepared to undergo great pain to have a collection that he didn't really care for.

Back at his house though, he was unsettled but happier than he had been in the hospital, thankfully! He had received a full medication review, just as we wanted and just as Andy needed. We had been allocated a community psychiatric nurse (CPN) called Dinah Robinson who was one of the few people that believed in us. Dinah, taking her life in her hands, would call every week at 9a.m. on a Tuesday to give Andy an injection of a mood stabilizer in his bottom. We normally had three staff around for this, for Dinah's protection. He still had to take some prescribed drugs (morning, afternoon and evening) and we were given PRN medication (for use when required), just in case his behaviour became unsustainable, with a diazepam base. Even with the medication in place though, his violence showed no sign abating.

Over time, Andy was doing more in the public sphere and was becoming know at certain public places, like the swimming baths, the bowling alley, various shops and eating places. The staff continued to have injuries, Andy continued to be restrained when absolutely, life-threateningly necessary and he continued with counting and putting his collections into towers or piles. He still made overtly sexual references, constantly masturbated in his room and cried now and again. It seems obvious why now, but at the time we did not put two and two together.

Powys Police

I had been married less than a year to Eamon who had booked a holiday to Las Vegas, which included a marriage at the Little White Chapel for my birthday in July - a complete surprise. We were married on the nineteenth of November 1998. Everything in life was on track and the business was being taken more seriously as people (that is, Social Services) began to realise how difficult Andy really was. I'm sure that most health professionals thought that I was exaggerating his behaviours - until they met him on a bad day, of course.

I was at Riversmead waiting for Andy to return with his staff when the phone rang. I answered it ('Hello, Scenario Management') and the answer came back, 'Can I speak to Barbara O'Donnell, please?' I said who I was, and the voice said that he was from Powys police and did I have a son called Andy who had attended Womaston School? I said I did, with a sinking feeling. The voice said, 'We have reason to believe that your son may have been sexually abused at the school by one or more male members of staff.'

I had seen scenes in film where the person being told terrible news sinks to the floor in disbelief. I thought this was a case of massive overacting. I actually slid down the work surface in the kitchen that I'd been leaning on and found myself on the kitchen floor as my legs gave way. I felt physically sick. My first thought was, 'Who was it?' I'd known all the staff at Womaston and really liked them. I asked who they were investigating, and they told me. I knew him well! He'd been one of the outreach team that had brought Andy back from Blackpool. A father of four, a grandfather and a husband and, I thought, a man to be trusted.

This all happened in seconds, though.

I answered the Powys police by asking them what their next move was. They asked if Andy was capable of giving evidence in court. I knew he wasn't. I told them about his limited capacity and his volatility and asked if they would take a statement from him instead. I said that I would make sure that the environment was safe; there would be three male, trained members of staff and me with Andy. I also told them that the questions they asked him had to be brief and easy to understand. If you said to Andy, 'have you had a good day?' - that would be a good question because of its simplicity – but if you said, 'What didn't you like about today?' - he would be totally flummoxed. There would be too many options for him. He would then have said anything or agreed to anything so that the person asking the questions would stop.

The police were reluctant to approach him, and they said that they would try and get statements from the other two children involved... Other two children! I asked if they could tell me which children they were, but all they could say was that there was another boy and a girl involved. There had been a boy and a girl in Andy's house at Womaston and they'd all been on a camping holiday before Andy was expelled.

When I got off the phone, I was beside myself with rage. I was so angry that I wanted to drive down to Womaston School and kill this man. But where would that leave Andy if I did? And what about my other children? There was nothing that I could do. It was the most frustrating and infuriating thing. I was so upset for Andy, so sorry for him. This, on top of everything else that life had thrown at him. It was so unfair, so cruel and so deviant. What a complete bastard, what a paedophile, what a bully. I was sobbing by this time and I knew that I had to keep up appearances and look happy for when Andy came back from his activity. So, I washed my face and waited for him to come back.

I made my children and the staff aware of what had happened so that we could address it and understand more of why he was so sexual and so aggressive. The police never did get back to me. The school closed in July 2014 after allegation of staff abuse to pupils. I found this out myself as I'd never stopped keeping an eye on the school. I was never told this news by anyone. I then contacted the Dyfed-Powys police and told them about Andy.

This experience couldn't have been more different. Two women officers came to talk to Andy and were confident, sensitive and kind to him. Although no arrests were made, they took us seriously and they did their best. They did not make us feel that because he was disabled, it didn't really matter – like they did in 1999.

New plans

It was during the period 1999 to 2002 that staff training was intensified as I had two clear plans. One was to query the amount that Andy was spending on his own care and whether this was actually legal and ethical. This had nothing to do with staff training but more to do with a feeling of mine that something about Andy's continuing self-funding was wrong. And secondly, to expand the bungalow to take in other people like Andy, who were deemed to be unplaceable, hence the training in all areas relevant to the people we supported.

For the first plan to come to fruition, I had to think where I would be able to find out about funding, regulations and law. This was in the days of non-reliance on computers. I had to go after work to the local library and study the Mental Health Acts (1984). I eventually came upon a chapter about the Section 3,117 (the one that Andy had been on in his three-month stay in the Psychiatric Ward at Victoria Hospital). It stated that if the patient needed 'aftercare' on his release from the Section, that is, have to be accompanied by care workers in the community because of his lack of capacity and assisted in day-to-day life because of his lack of ability to care for himself, then he should be paid for by the N.H.S. and Social Services. Joint funding was where the Social Care funding came from at the time.

And they'd known this all along!

They had clearly banked on me being thick, not doing my homework and by their actions, letting Andy's money disappear with no provision for his old age. I was absolutely furious but clear in what my next move would be. The next day, I phoned the Court of Protection to speak to Andy's Receiver, Pam. I told her the situation and within the week, the Court of Protection's solicitors were onto Lancashire County Council, demanding Andy's money back immediately on the promise of a tribunal, if this was not forthcoming.

Andy received a substantial amount back - all of it, in fact - and my reputation with Lancashire County Council was forever blackened.

I had put my idea of the expansion of Riversmead into a dormer bungalow to the Court of Protection and told them of my reasons why. The security of Andy staying supported in his own house was the main reason. If Andy shared his house with others with similar difficulties as himself, then it would be harder for the powers that be to close us down; they'd have more complex and dangerous people to rehouse. The Court of Protection agreed, as Andy's property would also be worth more, which made good business sense to their legal team.

Building went ahead for two more bedrooms and another shower room and toilet upstairs. Downstairs, another lounge was added and an additional toilet and shower room.

Lancashire County Council did not bargain for certain health professionals who believed in us and of our capabilities to take on the care of others with similar needs to Andy. These young adults would be on the autistic spectrum, have challenging behaviour, communication difficulties and with profound learning disabilities. The health professionals were Dr. Peter Fox (Clinical Psychologist) and Dinah Robinson, who had seen first-hand how determined we had been and how our hard work had paid off with Andy. They actively helped us by promoting us as a specialist service - which we were - and emphasised the fact that we had persevered with Andy, to his great improvement.

Then plan, number two, actually came together in 2003, when talks began with a mother from Preston whose son had been released from his school back into her care. He had been found to be so difficult by the staff of the school that they had blockaded him into his desk so that he couldn't get out and attack the other pupils, or them. He had communication problems and was non-verbal, challenging behaviour and was on the autistic spectrum. Perfect for us!

We were recommended by Dinah, supported by Dr. Peter Fox and the young man, Mr. D came to Riversmead on a twenty-four-hour care basis.

We had to fight for the funding for a 2:1 staff ratio in the daytime but we agreed with Social Services that he could share the 2:2 sleep-over staff with Andy. For the first month, we had used a waking watch because of the volatility of the new young man and the prospect of clashing with Andy, literally. No doubt, because of the strangeness of the new environment, being surrounded by strange, unfamiliar faces and the lack of the individual's communication skills there were many challenging moments.

We read everything we could about him: his past behaviours and what triggered them, his present behaviours and their triggers and he eventually settled. This was almost like a trial which we could not fail, as our reputation as amateurs would have been seen to be right. We had to win, and we did.

New individuals

Mr. D was complex and volatile, but we managed to discover his communication system. This was a customised version of Makaton signing invented by him, coupled with facial grimaces, leaping and running at people – then stopping dead. He also made noises and repeated certain sounds. That was his language. It was essential that we broke into his particular code. We eventually found out, after a lot of hard work and injury, what he liked to do for recreation (by a mixture of communication and family discussions) and what he liked to eat or didn't like to eat. Mr D. was extremely tactile and loved the feel of cuddly toys, all forms greenery and materials. He would also try to taste them, which his mother told us, was 'just his way'. Soon, Mr D. was getting out and about with his 2:1 staffing ratio – totally necessary – and was enjoying life.

When Dinah could see how we had progressed with Mr. D. she recommended us for another complex young man who was being supported by his lovely elderly grandparents and a care company that could not cope. This was in 2005. These grandparents were also looking after other family members that had been abandoned by the same parents. He did have a relationship with his father but not with his mother - unless the odd birthday card counts.

The poor grandparents were totally exhausted and needed support desperately. This young man, Mr. W., had been let down by the care company that Social Services had allocated him to, possibly because it was the cheapest option at the time. This company was using mainly - not all -untrained staff, who had no idea what to do as Mr. W was so complex and volatile.

We arranged for Mr. W. to visit Riversmead for a day out (picnic in the gardens, bouncy castle, and party food) and it went really well. He arrived with a member of staff that clearly liked him and was clearly trained. The staff member was impressed with our placement and asked us if Mr. W. did come to us, could he have a job so that he could come with him. Bonus!

When Mr. W. came to our placement permanently (if ever 'permanently' can be said of social care), he arrived with a few pieces of clothing, shoes, socks and underwear and a wardrobe. That was it. He had a bank account that had clearly been misused as there were five signees on it - and absolutely no available cash. His account was with the Royal Bank of Scotland and Andy's and Mr D.'s accounts were with Lloyds TSB (as was).There were very few daily logs available to view and no behaviour support plans. We got most of our information from the experienced care worker that came with him and members of his family.

I decided to become Mr. W.'s signee and move his bank to Lloyds TSB so as to make weekly transactions for the service users easier. As Mr. D. had before him, Mr. W. had to come into the bank, as proof of existence, with two support workers and myself, be asked questions that we encouraged him to answer without coercion. This was slightly fraught because of the constant threat of challenging behaviour but it was done successfully.

Before Mr D. arrived, social workers and other health professionals had ridiculed the idea that Andy could share his living space. One social worker had even suggested that it would only work if another kitchen was built at Riversmead so that the service users wouldn't mingle at all (!)

Inclusion eh?

Getting qualified

In 2003, I had decided that I needed to out-qualify the people that I went to meetings with. I felt, still, that I wasn't really being taken seriously because of the small size of the placement and the fact that I was Andy's mum. Between 2005 and 2008, I got qualified. I started my first degree and finished it in 2006. I did the degree concurrently with the Level 4 NVQ for the Registered Manager's Award and the Train the Trainer Award. I followed this with the Post Graduate Certificate of Education and then a master's degree in Contemporary Literature (this was for myself) which I completed in 2008. Meanwhile, I had completed the I.A.B.A. training and attended all the relevant courses associated with the workplace.

I was now able to run courses and to teach. I did a placement at Blackpool and the Fylde College (where I'd worked as a dinner lady 1992-93) and taught a foundation degree course entitled 'Understanding Specific Needs' and I was on the interview board at Lancaster University for the Clinical Psychology department (I still am). I felt that I should now be alright with the politically correct company who had never worked hands-on (those in work-based meetings) that I was forced to keep.

On the twelfth of March 2008, my mum died, just as I was finishing my master's degree. I had all the arrangements to do as my sister lived in Wales. I had cared for mum at her home until the dementia got too bad - and too dangerous for her to live alone. I then cared for her at my home for the last four years of her life (whilst I was finishing my first degree and during the PGCE and master's) with the help of two nurses that came for two hours morning and evening. They naturally had days off and holidays, so the rest of the care was all my responsibility. This was a hard time. I was still the Managing Director, Registered Manager and Signee for all the individuals that we supported. After Mr. W.'s woeful lack of funds when he arrived to be supported by us, I didn't really trust anyone on his behalf, so I got on with it. The same for Mr D. and of course, I was the Receiver and Financial Officer on behalf of Andy for the Public Trust Office.

From 1998 to 2008, lots of experience had been gained. The staff and I were helping other placements with people who were proving hard to support, so our reputation was getting good. We applied to support other people many times but were pipped at the post by the larger companies who were cheaper but whose staff were not as well trained.

During my education days, I had made enquiries into people with learning disabilities or autism who had become caught up in the prison system through no real fault of their own (for example, bullying, peer pressure, need to 'fit in', sexual and physical abuse that was copied). My idea was to be able to support them out of prison and include them into society as most of the institutions had been closed down or were closing – and there was nowhere for this group of people to go or be supported. I wanted to do a doctorate with this subject as my research area, but it was not to be. A mixture of no time, too expensive and exhaustion were the reasons.

Meanwhile, Social Services were making large financial cuts to the social care budget. We lost some of our staffing numbers, but I insisted that we needed a 2:1 staff to individual ratio in public, for safety's sake. I also insisted that we needed two sleep-overs – again for staff and personal safety. We really had to fight for this. Because the behaviours of each young man had improved, Social Services saw this as a reason to cut costs.

They didn't seem to think that if they cut daytime staff, then the individual's social mobility and hobbies would stop, then the behaviours would creep back up through lack of direction and boredom. I don't think they cared or saw the consequences of their proposed actions. They cared only for keeping their own jobs.

Local Recognition

Between 2008 and 2011, I think that I became known as a person that would not lie down and agree with everything that the professionals said. I was glad of this. If I had of over-respected the powers that be, Andy's money would have been used up on his care by this time or he would have been sectioned – no doubt under the cosh of heavy anti-psychotic medication – or he may even have died as a result of an accidental overdose or a restraint that went wrong.

There was another attempt to drastically cut the budget. I'd had enough by this time. I employed a solicitor that specialised in supporting people who had experienced negligence in the health and social care sector and people with learning disabilities who posed potential threats to their safety and others, all because of government financial cutbacks. The solicitor understood exactly the effect that cutbacks and therefore, lack of staff, would bring to the quality of life of the individuals we supported. He also understood the knock-on effect of the cutbacks, that there would be the return of behaviours we had modified by positive behavioural support and the inability (because of the lack of staff) to alter the direction of the individual's energies to another more positive place.

This solicitor worked for a large business in the Liverpool area, so not far away from our location in Thornton. Our company employed him, and we managed to keep our staffing levels. We did this by having him turn up unannounced to a meeting that had been previously arranged with Social Services, Social Workers, representatives of the Health Authority - and Nikky, and me. The presence of a solicitor made them seem nervous.

I think it came as a shock because, not only were they not expecting his presence, but it showed that I meant to keep the staffing and would fight by any means to do so. I was luckier than most people in a similar position, though, as Andy had received his large, monetary award. Without this award, I would have struggled to support him financially with legal backing.

Social Services seemed to be changing from a semi-protective, understanding role (on paper at least) to a body that questioned the necessity for staff, or that the over-staffing of a vulnerable person was directly linked to them being over-protected, unable to take minimal, everyday risks and being stifled in life and sociability. If we had gone along with their suggested cuts, the behaviours of our individuals would have deteriorated in public and in private.

Also, if anything had happened in the public sphere, we would have been blamed as a company and held to account as providing poor care. But that's what slashing the social care budget does - whilst it pretends that this minimal care is for the good of the individual - and the more money that is saved by the budget slashers, the more chance they have of keeping their extremely well-paid jobs.

On the seventeenth of March 2009, I was featured in the *Blackpool Evening Gazette* in an article named 'For Love of Andy.' Here it is:

Nothing is greater than a mother's love, but even the strongest bond is tested by tragedy.

Barbara O'Donnell has never given up on her son Andy, 29, no matter how difficult he has been.

Andy can be unpredictable and violent. Barbara has a dent in her face to prove it. "It was a kiss which changed into a head butt and fractured my cheekbone," she says, apportioning no blame.

Andy was a beautiful baby, bright and intelligent, when at fifteen months old, he suddenly became very poorly. Barbara, then living in Kent and pregnant with her third child, took him straight to her GP and was told he had a bad case of flu. By the following evening, he was no better and she phoned her doctor again. "He told me not to be silly. I was overreacting," she said.

She insisted on a home visit and a locum prescribed a different medication.

Next day, Andy rallied a little, but by the next day she knew there was something desperately wrong and rushed him to hospital. He had bacterial meningitis, the worst kind. He suffered fits, contracted pneumonia, and was left with seventy-five per cent brain damage, unable to walk, talk or feed himself.

"It was as if the old Andy was dead and that I'd been given a new baby, which, apart from looking same, was nothing like him," said Barbara, of Pembroke Avenue, North Shore.

Overnight, he had changed from a playful little boy into a terror, unable to reason or be reasoned with. Gone was the docile little boy, in his place, a child who liked to make as much noise as possible.

"I was told he was going to be a vegetable. He was seventy-five per cent brain damaged, but I was determined that he wouldn't be. I worked so hard to make sure he had a chance."

She got him walking, with a limp, talking and doing as much as he could for himself. Physically he improved, mentally he was irretrievably damaged.

The bigger he became, the more difficult it was for her to manage his bad behaviour.

When her marriage failed, Barbara, a mum-of-four, moved back to Blackpool where she would have the support of her own mother and family.

Andy went to school at Highfurlong Special School, Blackpool, until, at fourteen, he became so difficult to handle, she made the decision to let him go to a specialist residential school in Wales.

"Although they love him, my other children were frightened of him because he was so big and so strong. It was a very difficult situation. He was bigger and taller than me and was hitting people all the time. He would be up at 3am every day, shouting, whatever time he went to bed."

"I got used to existing on three hours' sleep a night, I was down to seven stone, had chickenpox followed by shingles and psoriasis.

"I couldn't not love him. I was protective of him. As much as he was violent, he was also vulnerable."

He was happy at boarding school for the first two years, his mum visiting regularly.

"But he moved from a reception area to the main house, which upset him, and in 1997, his dad died in a car accident and Andy went through the roof.

"It took five people to restrain him. His dad had loved him very much and visited him every month, Andy couldn't understand the concept of death. He went violent and started self-harming."

The school couldn't cope. Barbara was told that unless she found a care placement for him, he would be sectioned under the Mental Health Act.

Barbara knew no existing care facility would be prepared to take on her kid. "If he'd been sectioned, he would just have been fed drugs which I didn't want. I knew the only way was for me to drop everything and set up a care package."

Having successfully sued their former GP for failing to recognise meningitis, Barbara was able to apply to the Court of Protection for the release of some of the money awarded to Andy to buy a house in Thornton, in a rural setting, where he lives with round-the-clock care on a 2:1 basis, ensuring the safety of all involved.

Andy owns the house. Barbara, now qualified to a high level in specialist care, a trainer and assessor, set up a company, Scenario Management, to manage his care and to underpin it financially by providing residential care to another two young men, severely autistic and difficult to place.

The company employs a team of highly trained carers providing twenty-four-hour hour care to the young adults, like Andy, who have severe challenging behaviour, profound learning difficulties and autism.

"We take individuals who are very hard to place and give them support in a community setting," said Barbara. We are able to do this

because we have a highly experienced and well-trained staff team who undergo rigorous training to a high level.

"We also provide training in this specialist area," added Barbara, who is also mum to Caroline, 32, Bobby, 27 and Tommy, 26.

Barbara, married to former boxer Eamon Glennon since 1998 said: "All my children are fantastic. They are all great with Andy. I now visit him once a week. Like any 29-year-old, he doesn't want his mum breathing down his neck all the time. I know he likes to see me but he's very direct and will tell me when to go! He's happy, can go out with his carers and has a structured day."

Caroline and Bobby work with her at Scenario. "We've been on Lancashire County Council Preferred Providers List since 2004. As a company, there are a lot of hoops to jump through to get on this list, but it does mean that you have passed all the criteria needed to become a quality placement - and acceptable to the mainstream of course," she said.

With the introduction of direct payments, giving people who have been assessed as needing help from Social Services, to arrange their own care and support services instead of receiving them directly from the local council, Scenario has joined forces with other small Fylde independent care agencies, to form a consortium, Clip, to pool knowledge and expertise.

"We felt the care industry had lost its personal touch," said Barbara, who is passionate about the need to work closely with the person using their service, family, friends and other professionals to give individually tailored care packages.

Also, in Clip are Ormerod Home Trust, St Annes; the Willows, Cleveleys and Lord Durham, St Annes.

Things seemed to be going so well, for Andy and for the company.

Chapter 10

Surviving the Remodelling

Worrying Reviews

Before 2011, the company had also done domiciliary care in the community, helped out other companies who were struggling with a new, fairly unmanageable, individual and building up a name for ourselves. The staff were highly trained, either by me or by outside agencies and attended all the relevant courses to keep them up to speed with the latest legislation and ways of positively managing behaviours. We had built up a pretty good reputation. However, another cost-cutting initiative was instigated. Caroline and I attended it at Riversmead with two senior members of the staff. The result was that some hours were shaved off the packages of the young men we supported. This was not a drastic turn of events and we carried on.

Unfortunately, around 2011- 2013 (pre the Care Act and its practical implementation of 2014-2015), the ethos was to save money in the most drastic way. Instead of inclusion and individual treatment, the idea of large, instead of specialised, individualist companies, was been pushed. After years of training, telling everyone that people with a disability were all individuals and different – here they were saying that all disabled individuals should live under one roof, with drop-in care! Regardless of their differing disabilities. In other words, the institution system.

Even specialist villages for the disabled, not integration, was being pushed. This rang warning bells with me and other like-minded people in social care. It was clear that all those who wanted to keep their well-paid jobs were hastily agreeing. It was a real-life 'Emperor's New Clothes' situation. They gladly agreed with the Head of Social Services even though they can see the truth of the matter – that it made no common sense. Naturally, small companies were then targeted.

We were a small company. I had the reputation of taking no nonsense and that I would stand up for what I believed in. It was inevitable that we would get the expected phone call to meet up at County Hall, Preston to meet with a (Financial) Commissioner, Social Workers and the various Heads of Lancashire County Council. We did.

It was the first of October 2014 when I met with the 'Remodelling Team', a fancy title for people who were out to save money at the expense of vulnerable peoples' quality of life.

The Remodelling Team

I received a letter in August 2014 initially, from two young (and I mean about twenty-one years old) women Social Workers (one newly qualified, the other a RASO: a trainee social worker, therefore not even qualified) who were employed by the Remodelling Team. The letter informed me that they would be in touch with me soon to 'review.... the support you deliver to the service users we commission support for.' I smelled a rat straight away. The dead give-away was the phrase that, 'We commission support for.' Obviously, another cost cutting exercise but never before had I been so formally alerted by any Social Services department.

Every source of income was being looked into, as who the signee was and what their legal powers were. This all looks like a careful, open and honest process. It wasn't. It was an attempt to say that the people we supported - and had supported for years - were now 'cured' and could do more things for themselves. Their behaviours had miraculously disappeared over time and that they needed lots of time by themselves, without the interference and over-population of staff, which was holding them back socially and physically (the old 'deprivation of liberty' argument).

Of course, it was all about cutting costs and ruining the good work we had done over the last sixteen years. It was about money.

I had to be driven to the meeting by a staff member as I'd just had a hysterectomy operation and was supposed to be resting. At the meeting on the first of October, it was noticeable that the people present, the two young, just trained and incompletely trained social workers, a Just Checking representative (the company he represented sold electronic devices) and the Operational Manager of Lancashire County Council, all had very serious expressions. They made demands, rather than queries.

It was clear to me that they were going to reproduce a negative view of our company.

They said that the first impressions of the house were that it was over-populated with staff, that they wore lanyards – therefore emphasising the difference between staff and service-user – that the place was unkempt and that the social workers had been asked to hide or remove dangly earrings or necklaces as these may be targeted should the meeting get on the nerves of the individuals being supported. This was a genuine possibility, as the people we supported generally did not like new faces. (The 'social workers' etc. objected to this).

I was asked if I would show them in the next meeting the bank accounts of all three men. I was the signee for all, but I did nothing without asking or informing the individual's next of kin. So, I answered to that effect – yes, if the family and in my case, the Court of Protection agreed to this. They wanted to see all the outgoings, food, petrol, entertainment, household bills and all expenditure. They asked me for the first, but not the last, time if I had another job that I could go to. Then they asked if I was the Health and Welfare Guardian for Andy. I said yes, thinking that I was. In fact, I wasn't. I was the Receiver, the Financial Guardian, his Power of Attorney but not the Health and Welfare Officer.

Again, it was obvious what was going to happen – a financial exercise under the guise of giving the individuals we supported more responsibility. This was utterly ridiculous considering the individuals' lack of intellect, capability and their vulnerability. When I got home, I decided to check with the Court of Protection local office in the midlands, where you could always speak to a person, if I was already a Health and Welfare Officer. The man said, 'No, you're not.' I told him what was happening with Social Care cuts and he said, 'You'd better get the Health and Welfare Officer status as soon as possible, because if you don't, they can remove Andy to a cheaper placement, as they're paying for his upkeep.' I was horrified and asked him to send the forms to me as soon as he could, which he agreed to do.

The representative from Just Checking was due to make a visit. We were looking forward to this as a staff team. It was obvious that he had no idea of the clientele that he was dealing with. Alarm systems instead of staff for this area of care would be like assisted suicide. The day came and as we thought, the man was absolutely terrified, although he desperately tried to hide it. He had a rapid visit to see where he could put the alarms and epilepsy mattresses and then got out as quickly as he could.

Even though he had this experience, he still advocated that technology was the way forward as he was so desperate to keep his job at the expense of the vulnerable people that he was supposed to be protecting.

More Remodelling

The remodelling process remained in place, focussing on our placement for eighteen months, with the intention of closing it down. I cannot express just how awful it was and how much mail and email went between us, the Remodelling Team, the Court of Protection, the Solicitor and the Barrister. This part would be too lengthy - and boring, unless you were actively involved - but in that eighteen months:

- **I had a Safeguarding issue against me.**
  I had refused to let the Team know what was in Andy's current account, as advised by the Court of Protection.

- **The two just trained, not fully trained social workers called the police and said I was stealing from Mr. W.**
  They had been through all the individuals' cash and receipts - even though they were not the Audit Department of Lancashire County Council. We did not object, as we had nothing to hide. Mr. W. had been on holiday whilst I was in hospital having an operation and a discrepancy of just under £200 had been found from his holiday money receipts. The staff had apparently lost some receipts and could not account on paper for this amount, although they knew how it had been spent and I believed them. They'd worked with the company for the last ten years. But, although I had not been on the holiday, I was the signee and therefore to blame.

  When the policeman arrived, he made a joke of the situation asking, 'Shall I arrest her then?' Then saying to the social workers, 'Why aren't you reporting the staff that took the lad on holiday?'

- **The Remodelling Team's Social Worker had arranged for a Court of Protection Visitor to come to the house to prove that I was ripping off my son.**
  This action was another direct result of the refusal of the Team to have copies of Andy's current account and stocks and shares certificates, as advised by the Court of Protection. The Remodelling Team had clearly spoken to the Visitor beforehand, advising her that it would be in Andy's best interests to change placements. I guessed that I had been painted as a bad lot - which was obvious by the way she addressed me.

- **The Team said that sleepover staff weren't needed.**
  All three individuals had epilepsy, challenging behaviour and profound learning disabilities, plus erratic sleeping patterns. Apparently, the Just Checking Alarm system would suffice! (what if the alarm was broken, who would come, how long would it take? What if an individual had woken in the night and attacked another? What if one of the individuals had a profound seizure? How would an epilepsy mattress help if he died through lack of oxygen?) We'd allowed the system to be fitted at Riversmead, as we were compliant with most of their wishes - however unrealistic - but the alarm fittings had been dismantled and thrown out of the window by two of the individuals, so it was a pointless exercise. The epilepsy mattresses had been destroyed too.

- **They said that they needed to move Andy to another placement for his best interests.**
  Why? Andy owned his house. Unless of course they thought that they were going to move him as a foregone conclusion.

- **The staff were untrained.**
  A massive out-and-out lie.

- **Cutting down the staff first thing in the morning.**
  We were asked why we needed staff to come in at 8a.m. One of the supported men has double incontinence and sometimes refused to shower. Even though he could be covered in faeces, we would have to persuade him to wash himself, and this took patience and time. I was seriously asked, 'Why can't you wipe him down with a flannel or a wet wipe?

- **There was a secure numbered lock on the front door and Andy's bathroom was locked.**
  Some doors, like Andy's personal bathroom door, had to be locked as he had a habit of drinking the toilet water (used or un-used) with the intention of making himself sick. For example, when Andy had an episode of challenging behaviour, he was able to projectile vomit at staff as a means of control in an incident. If he wanted to go to the toilet, he would ask the staff, so he was not restricted in any way. The front door had to be securely locked as Mr. D. would run down the drive naked after his bath if it was open. And, anyway, who doesn't lock their front door?

- **The staff wore keys and lanyards creating the feel of an institution.**
  We wore lanyards because of the possibility of trouble in the public sphere. On occasion, the police had been called by a member of the public to separate what looked like a fight, or the police had been called to try to control an incident when we didn't wear lanyards.

- **Too many staff meant that they were restrictive.**
  The ability to safely go out for the day into the community with an appropriate number of staff members was lost on the Team.

- **The house was unfit for habitation and the trees in the drive were forbidding.**
  The house was always in constant repair because of the nature of the individuals we supported. The trees gave some privacy to the building. Nevertheless, we complied and had the lovely trees chopped down. And redecorated, yet again.

- **There was a conflict of interest with me being mum, signee, Receiver and Financial Officer for Andy – and being the Managing Director and Registered Manager of Scenario Management.**
  This had never bothered them for the last sixteen years when we had taken on emergency placements or helped out other companies with our staff and permanently housed Mr. W. and Mr. D.

It was clear that they wanted any excuse to shut us down.

Much More Remodelling

I had recently persuaded the Court of Protection to allow Andy's fund to buy another property across the road from Andy. The last of the 'institutions' were being closed down in Lancashire and potentially dangerous individuals were being relocated into society. I saw this as an opportunity for some people to have good care and integration back into the community – and it was also good business sense for Andy, as stocks and shares were not performing as well as rents. The Court agreed with me.

I was constantly asked by one of the Remodelling Team, 'Do you have another job to go to?' or 'Do you have another form of income?' Also, 'Do you really think that you will be able to support other individuals in the new house?' These questions were clear indications that they were going to put me out of a job, close the business and were questioning the competency of our supporting other people. I kept calm, but inside I was planning my moves – and I was enraged.

I started by asking the Court of Protection if the Visitor had spoken to the Remodelling Team before coming to the house. They said they'd phone me back with information.

They did. Apparently, the main social workers and 'Best Interest' people with the Team had a long meeting with the Visitor before she met me, painting me to be a criminal who was after her son's money and that it was advisable that he should be supported elsewhere. I asked the Court of Protection team if I could access the report by the Visitor. They let me have a copy of it and it was exactly as I thought it would be. I was made to look like I was on the make. It was infuriating.

I then asked if I could now have an impartial Visitor from the Court of Protection and said that one who had some life experience would be preferable, rather than a pen-pusher with only a little experience of our area of care. The Court of Protection were pretty appalled at what was going on - especially about the real agenda of the Remodelling Team which was becoming more and more apparent - so they said that they'd get another Visitor in place as soon as they could.

This happened two weeks after the first Visitor and this time, she didn't fire questions at me or treat me with a lack of respect, but she listened to what I had to say and checked the works' paperwork. She had experience of this area of care and totally understood how hard it was. She observed the staff team, asked them some questions and made her report - which was completely different from the 1st Visitor's account in its positivity.

The Court of Protection contacted one of the Best Interest social workers and said that there was no problem with the way that I ran Andy's current account and that there never had been in all the years that I had been the Receiver.

Unfortunately, this information was not relayed to the Care Quality Commission as it should have been (the Best Interest team had decided not to tell them). I therefore still had a Safeguarding concern against my name. I had to really persist in having it removed. It was the first time that our Care Quality report had identified more 'needs improvement' than 'good'. I was infuriated.

This was an awful time. The staff were upset about the way they were treated (drop-in visits, no doubt to try and catch us out, by Social Services staff - and the Just Checking electronics man - all of whom refused to sign the Visitors Book). We were bullied and attempts were made to intimidate myself and the staff. We were all treated as if we didn't know what we were doing, and we were thoroughly fed up and angry. Our hours had been slashed, staff had been injured and all our hard work was beginning to look like it had been for nothing.

Mr. D.'s mother (who was very ill) had been approached by a Best Interest social worker and asked if she would like Mr. D. to be rehoused nearer to her. She only lived eighteen miles away anyway in Preston and already had regular contact with Mr. D. through our staff. She said 'yes' just to get rid of the social worker - Mrs. D. phoned me and told me this herself. She died four months later.

I had been banned from all the other Best Interest meetings, a fact that I couldn't wait to relay to my solicitor. It was actually illegal to ban me as these were individuals under my care and support and I should have been able to give my input. Caroline and I attended the Best Interest meeting for Andy.

Caroline had had an operation only a couple of days before the meeting and was very tired and quite poorly – but she insisted on attending. The meeting was full of the usual suspects, along with a Safeguarding Officer, two members of the N.H.S., a solicitor for Lancashire County Council and Andy's doctor. As the meeting progressed, it was obvious that the N.H.S., Andy's doctor and even the Lancashire County Council solicitor were leaning towards us as the Remodelling Team's evidence of needing less staff and all their other complaints began to look more and more flimsy.

Even the write-up of the Best Interest meeting for Andy was incorrect when we received it a few days later. It said that Andy had been to school in Paris not Powys (!) and throughout the document, Andy was referred to by another of our service user's names. It was an obvious cut and paste job.

Because the Court of Protection had been involved and knew what was really going on, they approved the funding for a Judicial Review, using the same solicitor that we'd used before on the last cost-cutting exercise. All of our correspondence (between us and the Remodelling Team) was given to our solicitor and it was sent to the barrister in London. The Court of Protection meant business and so did we.

Needless to say, we won. All the stolen hours that had been taken out of the care packages were reinstated. The Best Interest meetings that the Remodelling Team held for all of the service users were for nothing as the Deprivation of Liberty Safeguard Act's (D.o.L.S.) cases of the individuals had not even been heard yet in the Court or even approved. Surely, the Remodelling Team should have known that they were acting illegally? It was all scare tactics to get us to close down. The Remodelling Team were made to look foolish and unprofessional, not to mention heartless and cruel. The older women in the team all had children – a fact that I found hard to believe, considering what they were trying to do with mine.

Strangely, they all took on new jobs and the Team was disbanded – but I'm sure that it will spring up again under a different name, but with the same goal, saving money.

Epilogue

And Now

Enough is enough

After this last experience, I'd had enough. For nearly eighteen years, I'd had to go to meetings with people who liked the sound of their own voices and never delivered what they'd said. People who were at a meeting and couldn't wait to plan the next meeting. People who advocated the minimum wage for carers yet drove around in 4 x 4's.

I was sick of saying at meetings, 'Care will never be taken seriously as a career choice unless pay, conditions and training are improved upon. Until then, care staff are seen, and will continue to be seen, as skivvies. Workers packing the shelves at Lidl get paid more than care workers – and which is more important?'... etc. etc. etc. and always being ignored when I said the speech.

Most, not all, of the people in these meetings were people who I would have crossed the road to avoid. People who had no hands-on experience who advised care staff what to do in a moment of crisis – the same people who, when a crisis happened, would be first out of the door. People who let politically correct language bias their thinking. People with no shred of common sense. People who were desperate to keep their jobs.

They were making me ill, quite literally. In 2012, I had a T.I.A. mini stroke, followed by another one about six months later. My body was trying to tell me that enough was enough. I was also exhausted, as was Bobby. He had worked with Andy's staff – and other care companies – on and off, since 1997 until 2017, when he became burnt out with challenging behaviour. If it hadn't been for his hands-on work in those early days (as well as Nikky and the two Pauls) and taking many a beating in my place, I doubt if we'd have succeeded as a care company. Tommy recently visited Andy, with his wife

Jin and the visit, after many years of not seeing Andy, was a total success. Bobby is a successful D.J. based in Leeds and Tommy is an executive in Manchester.

I am still involved in staff training and giving talks about positive life experiences to trainee Clinical Psychologists at Lancaster University. I am still Managing Director of Scenario Management but since Caroline has taken over the role of Registered Manager, she has made a real success of it. We have expanded beyond belief in the years that she has been in charge – I knew I wasn't taken seriously! – and it carries on doing so under her guidance. The future looks positive; for everyone.

And now... Andy continues his enjoyment of life. Obviously, he still has moments of violence and conflict as do most of the people we support, and his epilepsy will always be present - but he enjoys going on holiday and still loves his collections of Mr. Men and Little Miss books and his collection of Roses chocolate tubs. He likes his Ladybird books too – but not as much as his Mr. Men.

He is still over-excited at birthdays and at Christmas, but this will always be the case. His right-side hemiplegia is more evident as time has gone by and he walks with a pronounced limp. He needs to go out in a wheelchair when he goes into the community as he tires easily. His medication has made him gain weight, as has his lack of movement. He does not let this hold him back in life! He loves his food, his possessions, his D.V.D's and his staff who he has an excellent relationship with. I visit – for my regular 'mum visit' every week and we have a good laugh together.

Andy is now forty. His prognosis was that he would live no longer than his thirties. I am glad that I did what I did; even though it was hard, sometimes painful and sometimes incredibly funny. I know that Andy is safe - and that means everything to me, Caroline, Bobby and Tommy.